**IN THE
OF 1
SANDW...**

D0387474

Open style. Served with creamy cole slaw

NOSH, NOSH NANETTE Hot turkey, with gravy,
cranberry sauce, French fried potatoes
or baked beans 19.95
BEEFAMANIA Hot roast beef, with gravy,
French fried potatoes or baked beans 19.95
LI'L ABNER Hot brisket of beef, with gravy,
French fried potatoes or baked beans 19.95
HAMALOT Hot Virginia ham, with gravy,
candied sweets or baked beans 19.95

SHARING - $3.00 EXTRA

deli & egg
sandwiches
(3) Three Eggs

Delicatessen omelette sandwich	8.95
Corned beef and egg sandwich	9.95
Tongue and egg sandwich	9.95
Pastrami and egg sandwich	9.95
Salami and egg sandwich	8.95
Bologna and egg sandwich	8.95
Ham and egg sandwich	9.95
Western sandwich	8.95
Bacon and egg sandwich	9.95
Egg sandwich	7.45

Cheese on sandwich extra 2.00

NOT FOR MEAT EATERS BUT FOR
THE BIG "FRESSER" OR FOR TWO (2) TO SHARE
MILTON'S SMORGASBORD
Four (4) freshly baked miniature rolls individually
stuffed with shrimp salad, tuna salad, chicken salad,
and egg salad served with raw onion, lettuce and
tomato slices and sweet red pepper.
22.45

How to Feed Friends
and Influence People

How to Feed Friends and Influence People

THE CARNEGIE DELI

A GIANT SANDWICH, A LITTLE DELI, A HUGE SUCCESS

MILTON PARKER
Owner of The Carnegie Deli
AND ALLYN FREEMAN

WILEY

JOHN WILEY & SONS, INC.

Published by John Wiley & Sons, Inc., Hoboken, New Jersey.
Published simultaneously in Canada.

For general information on our other products and services please contact our Customer Care Department within the United States at (800) 762-2974, outside the United States at (317) 572-3993 or fax (317) 572-4002.

Wiley also publishes its books in a variety of electronic formats. Some content that appears in print may not be available in electronic books. For more information about Wiley products, visit our web site at www.wiley.com.

Library of Congress Cataloging-in-Publication Data:

Parker, Milton, 1919–
  How to feed friends and influence people: the Carnegie Deli—a giant sandwich, a little deli, a huge success / Milton Parker, Allyn Freeman.
    p. cm.
  ISBN 0-471-68056-7 (cloth)
  1. Carnegie Deli (Restaurant). 2. Cookery, Jewish. I. Freeman, Allyn.
II. Title.
  TX945.5.C35P37   2005
  641.5′09747′1—dc22   2004016487

Printed in the United States of America.

10 9 8 7 6 5 4 3 2 1

CONTENTS

ACKNOWLEDGMENTS

With Love from CARNEGIE DELICATESSEN & RESTAURANT

The authors wish to thank the following people who helped with this book:

- *Carnegie Deli Management:* Sandy Levine encouraged the work from the beginning and was particularly cooperative making information available and scheduling staff interviews. Jeff Jensen gave instructive Commissary tours, provided recipes, and was helpful with cured meat information. Marian Parker Levine supplied wonderful anecdotes. Others who lent a hand were Irving Parker, Henry Carlen, and Patricia Cruz.
- *Carnegie Deli Staff:* Foremost is waiter Jack Sirota who supplied stories old and new and related celebrity tales. Other staff interviewed who shared memories were Cook Fernando Perez, Senior Counterman Walter Bell, and Servers Wayne Lammers, Muriel Caraballo, Susan Palmaccio, Rasmee Ruenanukool, and Annie Smith. Valuable information came from Kay Siricharoen and Cook Mickey Ayala. Thanks to everyone else at the Carnegie Deli and the Commissary.
- *Old Memories:* Herbert Hudes and Ilene Hudes Deines.
- *Luminary Interviews:* We are indebted to Joel Siegel at ABC and Bob Simon at CBS. Special appreciation to Mimi Sheraton, who graciously recalled Leo Steiner memories. Noted attorney Raoul Felder was also helpful. Rabbi Alvin Kass recounted two superb stories.
- *Restaurateurs and Food People:* Heartfelt thanks to Bob Orzo of Hudson Bagels and to Bal Golden, former owner of the Assembly Steak House. At Omaha Steaks, Steve Simon, Jackie

Thompson, and Beth Weiss offered memories and helpful information. We picked a peck of pickle stories from Steve Leibowitz at United Pickle Company.

- *Media:* We are grateful to writers Steve Viuker and Jennifer Nelson, and photographers Nanine Hartzenbusch and Pete Levin.
- *Deli Maven:* Composer Michael Isaacson was on hand 24/7 for questions about deli food and deli decor. His Brooklyn Egg Cream recipe can be found inside the book.
- *Friends:* Attorney Fred Waxman deserves special consideration. Encouragement came also from Ruth Mills, Janice Lee, Susan and Richard Lewis, Ann and Bob Gorman, Mardee Cavallero, Judy Goldsmith, Steve Berkenfeld, Pat and Charles Clarkson, Deanie and Jay Stein, Carrie and Bill Rosenthal, Ann Patch, Cynthia Jenner, Carol and Martin Taffet, Marcia Shrock, Laura and Doug Fielding, Fran Panasci, Nicole Davis, John Clarkson, The Murphy Clan of Dingle, Deb Green, Bob Golden, Kathy Green, Rochelle and John Schofield, Marian and Ted Last, Diane Kane Yamada, Hunan Pan, Sazerac House, and appreciative resident deli tasters, Jeff Chase and Basil di Cano.
- *John Wiley & Sons, Inc.:* The book was the brilliant idea of Senior Editor Matt Holt to whom all praise is due. Tamara Hummel offered wonderful assistance. Jo-Ann Wasserman maintained a keen deli interest throughout. Linda Indig managed the production of the book from start to finish.

From Milton Parker: Special gratitude to my wife Mildred, son Jeffery, daughter Marian, and granddaughter Sarri.

From Allyn Freeman: Without founder Milton Parker, there would be no Carnegie Deli today and no Carnegie Deli book. A warm thank you to Sandy, Marian, Jeff, and the entire deli staff. And special thanks to Chuck Smith.

How to Feed Friends and Influence People

DOING BUSINESS THE CARNEGIE DELI WAY

The Carnegie Deli has become a successful commercial enterprise because it has operated on sound business principles. Today, it is an internationally recognized brand known to both New Yorkers and tourists as a must stop.

In 1937, the deli embarked on a 67-year journey to progress from a modest 92-seat restaurant to a national award-winning delicatessen. It has been featured prominently and often on the Food Channel cable network, television shows, and also in domestic and foreign magazines and newspapers. When the media want to wax nostalgic about delicatessen food, the Carnegie Deli always comes to mind.

Leo Steiner and Milton Parker, the partners responsible for the restaurant's success, had no million-dollar revenue stars in their eyes. Their initial goal was simple: to make a decent profit at the end of the day. Parker has said, "If we were left with more cash at the end of the week, we considered the deli a success."

Of the more than 300 New York-area delis in 1976, when the Carnegie changed hands, only 30 exist today because dining tastes changed over time. In addition, a delicatessen, if run correctly (like the Carnegie), is a 22½-hours-a-day, hands-on operation. Few new restaurateurs have elected to make delicatessen work their life's profession.

CARNEGIE DELI: BUSINESS 101

What business guidelines has the deli employed over these many years? What are the keys to its commercial success? Why did it survive when so many other famous New York City delicatessens (e.g., The Madison Avenue Deli, Wolfs on West 57th Street) faded into obscurity?

At the outset, the Carnegie Deli—a multimillion-dollar operation—has no thick book that contains a Mission Statement or an elaborate, numbers-driven business plan. Current management never speaks of "company culture" or "core competency." The deli sticks to basic business principles.

It follows 10 straightforward business practices:

1. *Keep it simple.* The Carnegie Deli's product is delicatessen food and only deli food.
2. *Do one thing better than anyone else.* Customers have a choice where to eat deli in New York City, so the Carnegie consistently succeeds in serving a higher-quality, better-tasting, and larger-portion product than any other competitor.
3. *Create a family atmosphere among the staff.* Time and time again, the staff, many who have been working at the Carnegie for 15 years or more, use the phrase, "We're family here."
4. *Promote from within.* The deli grooms people to fill the slots when workers retire. The upper, supervisory levels of the staff (cooks, countermen, servers) started out at the lowest rank.

5. *Have an open ear to staff and customer comments.* At the deli or at the commissary, senior management are constantly asking customers and wholesale clients about quality. In addition, the staff know they can discuss matters with management in an open and free exchange.

6. *Make it yourself.* The Carnegie commissary cures, pickles, and smokes its own fresh meats and bakes its pastries daily. The deli also purchases only high-quality fresh bread, pickles, and so on, from leading suppliers.

7. *Own the premises.* The Carnegie owns the building on Seventh Avenue and the 22,000-square-foot commissary in New Jersey.

8. *Management is always responsible.* There's no finger-pointing. If something goes wrong or is mishandled, management is at fault.

9. *Do not be greedy.* The Carnegie Deli could license its name for similar products that could be made by other food companies. But the Carnegie insists that only products made in its own commissary will be sold at retail or wholesale.

10. *Have fun working.* The staff at the deli and at the commissary enjoys coming to work. They're happy to be part of the Carnegie Deli family.

There are many business decisions—most profitable, others less so—that contributed to the Carnegie's success. Attempts to open branches in other cities have failed. The original commissary in downtown Manhattan (a leased arrangement that supplied only the deli) eventually became a Carnegie Deli-owned, 22,000-square-foot plant that now accommodates all of the wholesale and retail demands.

The growth of the Carnegie Deli is a Cinderella business story, starting out as a plain, nondescript, hole-in-the-wall restaurant and emerging as the delicatessen of choice for

A CHRONOLOGY OF JEWISH OR DELI FOOD IN THE USA

Year	Location	Event
1862	New York	Gulden's Mustard
1869	New York	Dr. Brown's Cel-Ray Tonic
1870	Cincinnati	Fleischmann's Yeast
1870	New York	Rokeach Kosher Foods
1872	Chester, NY	Cream cheese (Philadelphia brand in 1880)
1883	New York	Horowitz Matzos* Bakery
1887	Cincinnati	Manischewitz Matzos*
1888	New York	Breakstone Dairy Store
1888	New York	Katz's Delicatessen
1905	New York	Hebrew National Foods
1905	New York	Ratner's Dairy Restaurant
1908	New York	Barney Greengrass, the Sturgeon King
1908	Providence, RI	Sanford Friedman born†
1910	New York	Yonah Schimmel Knishes
1914	New York	Russ and Daughters Appetizers
1916	New York	Streit's Matzos*
1916	Brooklyn	Nathan's Hot Dogs
1921	New York	Leo Linderman opens Lindy's (cheesecake)
1927	New Haven	Lender's Bagel Bakery
1931	Los Angeles	Canter's Delicatessen
1933	California	Mogen-David Wines
1934	Brooklyn	Monarch Wine
1937	**New York**	**Carnegie Delicatessen**
1937	New York	Stage Delicatessen
1940	New York	Barton's Candy Store
1945	Beverly Hills	Nate 'n Al's Delicatessen
1950	Brooklyn	Junior's Delicatessen
1954	New York	Second Avenue Delicatessen
1972	New York	H&H Bagels

*Although Matzoh is spelled with an "h" on the official deli menu, these brands are as trademarked.
†Sanford Friedman traveled extensively throughout the Northeast and Midwest from 1945 to 1985. After eating in many delicatessens, his sage advice was, "Never order deli north of West 96th Street, west of the Carnegie Deli on Seventh Avenue, east of Avenue D on the Lower East Side, or south of Delancey Street."

presidents, celebrities, one sultan, and, most importantly and profitably, the world's delicatessen eating public.

The first Carnegie Deli opened in 1937 in a small interior space. It started without pretensions, just another deli in the West Fifties, an area made more famous by the 1931 construction of Rockefeller Center (not completed until 1940). The sprawling office, retail, and cultural complex changed forever the dowdy tenement look of the area.

There are many famous restaurants in the United States, but there is only one Carnegie Deli. This book narrates its marvelous tale.

1937: THE OPENING

The location: 854 Seventh Avenue near West 55th Street in Manhattan. In 1937, the building code for the area changed to permit retail establishments at street level in former residential buildings. Soon after, Seventh Avenue south of West 57th Street started to attract more retail stores.

The event: Izzie and Ida Orgel opened a 40-seat restaurant, which they named the Carnegie Deli because of its proximity to Carnegie Hall. In those days, it was typical for Manhattan retail establishments to name themselves after nearby landmarks. Today, Milton Parker jokes, saying, "They named a world famous concert hall after *us*."

The restaurant featured a small kitchen and a dining room counter for making sandwiches. The cuisine consisted of Eastern European/Jewish deli food: cured meat sandwiches, hot brisket or flanken, chicken in the pot, chopped liver, matzoh ball soup, and apple strudel or rice pudding for dessert. Sandwiches were 50 cents.

Seven blocks downtown on West 48th Street and one west on Broadway, another 40-seat restaurant opened in 1937. It was called the Stage Delicatessen because of its proximity to the Broadway theaters.

The original clientele at the Carnegie Deli consisted of local residents and musicians and performers at Carnegie Hall who dined before or after practice, or for dinner before a concert. Since many of the customers were European, it was a treat to have familiar deli cuisine near the great hall.

No one on March 11, 1937, regarded the opening of this delicatessen as a memorable date in the history of New York City. It was just another deli, one of hundreds in the five boroughs of New York.

1942 TO 1976: CARNEGIE MAX HUDES

In 1942, the Orgel family sold the Carnegie Deli to Max Hudes, who had operated a takeout-only delicatessen at Broadway and West 103rd Street. He wanted a sit-down delicatessen and was attracted by the Carnegie's midtown location.

In the 1950s, the major TV studios and sound stages were a few blocks downtown in Manhattan's West Fifties. Many show business performers, pals of Max's from his boyhood growing up in the Bronx, would come over from the Ed Sullivan, Sid Caesar, and Jackie Gleason shows.

To promote the deli, Hudes relied on radio advertising. Some old-timers can still remember the commercials on Long John Nebel's program, touting the great food. Some remember the matchbooks with the caricature of "Carnegie Max."

The Carnegie had to respond to the competition from the Stage Deli, which had moved uptown, to Seventh Avenue and West 54th Street, in 1942. The Stage was run by the legendary Max Asnas, who made his place the spot for showbiz and sports celebrities.

In the 1960s, the Carnegie catered the Sunday morning dress rehearsals of the British rock invasion. Max's son Herbert can remember taking coffee, bagels, and Danish to the Beatles and the Rolling Stones. The bands stayed at hotels in the area and would come into the Carnegie after their performances.

By 1976, Max Hudes and his two partners had aged. They had tried for two years to sell the delicatessen and the building but without success. They asked some restaurant brokers to help find new ownership. After 34 years operating the second incarnation of the Carnegie Deli, it was time for new owner-ship and new directions.

1976: The Deli House That Leo and Milton Built

In December 1976, the new owners' primary goal was to gen-erate more business. The revenues had fallen off significantly during the two years that the Carnegie had been up for sale.

The plan was to offer the same deli fare as the then more fa-mous Stage Deli, a block south on the same, west side of Sev-enth Avenue. But there were two notable exceptions: the Carnegie Deli would hand cure its three top-selling sandwich meats—pastrami, corned beef, and tongue—and not buy whole-sale like the Stage; and the Carnegie would not compete with the Stage's famous show business-named sandwiches.

"We'll keep it simple," said Leo Steiner to Milton Parker.

"That's okay with me," replied Parker.

Steiner hired his brother Sam to begin curing meats in the basement with a hand-pumped brine machine. This was a labor-intensive method for injecting a secret pickling solution (to ten-derize the meat). The meats were left to cure and pickle for 7 to 10 days to produce the distinctive flavor. After pickling, the meats were boiled for up to three hours and then brought di-rectly to the counter for steaming. Afterward, they were sliced hot onto bread and then served to the customers.

Milton Parker made a mental note that when business im-proved, he would change the old Carnegie Deli's blinking neon sign with its pale yellow background. It looked like an old style neon sign from the 1930s era of Times Square.

Years came and went, but the sign never changed. Today, it is a nostalgic reminder of the old days, one of the last blinking neon signs in Manhattan.

Over the next 28 years, the pale yellow backdrop and the scripted sign would welcome millions of diners. But on that December day in 1976, the owners had no knowledge of what the future of the Carnegie Deli would be.

They only knew it was time to go to work.

1979: You're the Tops!

On March 2, 1979, readers of the *New York Times* Friday Weekend section were at first surprised and then captivated by a six-column article spreading across page C16. It was a review written by Mimi Sheraton, the dean of New York City's influential newspaper and magazine food critics. The headline grabbed everyone's attention: "Where to Eat the Best Pastrami and Corned Beef in Town."

The article, almost as lengthy as but more gripping than a short story, captured readers' attention the way no other food critic's column had ever done before or would ever do again. The reason was evident: The food mentioned, the food being rated, the prizes being awarded were not to fancy restaurants serving haute or nouvelle cuisine. Sheraton had not graded the best foie gras, the tastiest risotto Milanese, or the most delicious white truffles. She had rated the most democratic of New York City restaurant favorites: delicatessen pastrami and corned beef.

New Yorkers prided themselves on their deli experiences and were often competitive when declaring their earliest deli meals:

- "I was nine months old when I ate in a deli."
- "Oh, yeah. I was conceived minutes after my parents left the deli."
- "Big deal. I was born on the floor of a deli."

In discussions of cured meats in this town, everyone had an opinion, and everyone had a favorite deli. And who, New Yorkers wondered as they scanned the headline in the *Times*, had been named the town's pastrami and corned beef winners? Which of the 16 Metropolitan New York delis rated were the champs or the chumps?

Sheraton had eschewed the paper's four-star, best-place ranking for a more down-to-earth best rating called simply, "The Tops." Three delicatessens were cited in this top-of-the-line category.

The Pastrami King was located in Kew Gardens, Queens, which to Manhattanites could have been Podunk or Pawtucket it was so far away. The second deli was in Manhattan, Bernstein's-on-Essex Street. This was the legendary Lower East Side restaurant that served a combination of delicatessen and kosher Chinese food. Here, the waiters wore tasseled Chinese skullcaps or *yarmulkes*. But Essex Street was on the Lower East Side in a part of the city most people had forgotten about. And the odd mishmash of kosher and Chinese did not say "all deli all the time."

The third of the "Tops" turned out to be a revelation for deli-discriminating Manhattan tastes. It was the known, but unknown, Carnegie Deli on Seventh Avenue, located in the heart of upper midtown. It had always been referred to as the "other" deli, the one up the street from the Stage.

In the true meaning of the quintessential New York second, at 11 A.M. the Carnegie, a restaurant that had been revitalized by its new owners two years earlier with no notice taken by the deli-eating public, witnessed its first-ever line of people clamoring to get in. As the day continued, the line grew and grew and grew as New Yorkers, many clutching the *Times* article in their hands, awaited their turn to taste (and to judge, of course) the cured meats, but especially the pastrami.

On that Friday, March 2, 1979, the world of the Carnegie Deli changed in dramatic and astonishing ways its two owners could never have imagined. It was like a *Times* theater critic giving a rave review to a Broadway show. There was one substantial difference, though. Not everyone attended the theater, but everyone ate and loved deli.

An actress-turned-professor from Chicago who remembered the review said, "It was the classic theatrical tale of the unknown chorus girl stepping out of the back line to take over the star's role and receive a standing ovation."

Twenty-five years later, that initial magnificent review continues to inspire the Carnegie Deli. The lines that formed on that Friday in 1979 still form every day, and the cured meats remain the best tasting.

Bernstein's-on-Essex closed in 1988, and by 2004 the Pastrami King was only a memory in Queens. This left the Carnegie Deli as the last of the three fabulous "Tops."

Mimi Sheraton and the New York Times

Turn back the clock to 1979. The *New York Times* was one of the few serious local guides to dining spots in the city. Starting in 1957, when Craig Claiborne realized a lifelong ambition to become the *Times* restaurant critic, the newspaper treated dining and new restaurants with almost the same importance as the openings of Broadway shows. The city's middle and higher income classes, who dined out often and well, considered the newspaper's one- to four-star review as the definitive restaurant guide.

In 1976, Brooklyn-born Mimi Sheraton assumed the stewardship of the *Times* food and restaurant column. She was the daughter of a commission merchant in a wholesale produce market and of a mother who was an excellent cook.

From the outset, as Sheraton demonstrated an openness to taste all types of foods, she attracted readers to her Friday Weekend column. She expanded the scope of her restaurant reporting, going beyond reviewing only fancy European dining spots. She always visited a restaurant incognito, and at least three times to ensure that a hit or miss was not based on one good or one bad dining experience.

Most of her reviews—using the same four-star system—rated multinational cuisines or smaller restaurants. For Sheraton, the how and why of preparation remained vital, whether she was eating the food of a French chef with a Cordon Bleu degree or of a cook from Sicily, serving up his island's peasant fare.

Her egalitarian approach resulted in reviews of many cuisines in every section of Manhattan, and in the four outer boroughs—an innovative attitude at the time. If a Moldavian bistro opened in Forest Hills, Queens, or a Tasmanian eating place opened in Williamsburg, Brooklyn, Sheraton would dine there many times to rate it. In the past, she had reviewed New York's Chinese restaurants that served kosher food and the kitschy Sammy's Roumanian Steakhouse on the Lower East Side.

Sheraton added interesting tidbits to her columns, citing the history and preparation of ingredients. Her writing proved enlightening and honest. Mimi Sheraton was a New York native whose reviews were trustworthy. To New Yorkers, her word was true, and the *Times* was the paper of record.

The Review

The article that greeted readers on that Friday was sizable, covering six columns, the maximum width of the broadsheet, and it totaled about 2,500 words. It featured a large black-and-white cartoon by Niculae Asciu of a chef slicing stacks of the word *PASTRAMI* and placing the letters on bread (understood to be rye). Every detail of the article shouted, "Important New York food communication. Read this."

In the first half of the article, readers learned the history of the age-old, time-tested preparation of processing pastrami and corned beef. Sheraton wrote about the esoteric names for two different cuts of pastrami (deckle and plate) and revealed much about the time-consuming methods to perfect the right seasoning, the importance and technique of steaming, and the prerequisite of hand slicing (to allow for the spices to tumble onto the meat), and the final "must-do"—serve the cured meats hot.

Readers' mouths watered as the critic wrote, "Pastrami is cured exactly like corned beef, but it is then dried and rubbed with a heavy mixture of coarse, black butcher pepper, other spices, and often with crushed fresh garlic."

But the column also cited numerous shocking facts about the local making of cured meats. Sheraton told the story in *J'Accuse* detail. Few of the 16 delis rated cured their own pastrami or corned beef. Most bought from a single outside supplier, whose quality varied from sale to sale and week to week. But more scandalous was the revelation that some delis employed shortcuts to quick smoke the pastrami, which resulted in an acrid aftertaste. The most egregious detail was that some delis manipulated the true size of a sandwich by using smaller slices of bread and deceitful meat layering techniques. (What was the New York deli world coming to?)

She also weighed all the sandwiches, checking 104 of them on a single day. At the bottom of each deli's review, readers saw the price for the sandwiches and the true sandwich weights.

Fortunately, Sheraton confirmed that there still remained cured meat purists in New York, skilled and dedicated practitioners in the art of making quality pastrami and corned beef. Some delicatessens emphasized Old World quality. A few places survived, like the Carnegie Deli, that prepared and hand-cured meat to perfection.

Lines at the Carnegie

A few days prior to the *Times* review, Mimi Sheraton introduced herself to Leo Steiner. She told him that she had dined five times at the Carnegie and hinted that the upcoming Friday article would bring customers in by the droves.

Later, after she left, the two owners stared at each other; they had never been reviewed by a publication as prestigious as the *New York Times*. Could Sheraton be telling the truth: that hundreds, maybe thousands of deli lovers would be lining up at the Carnegie's front door? Could a newspaper review of cured meats change the deli dining preferences of finicky New Yorkers?

The Carnegie had been selling lots of pastrami weekly. It had to gear up for the possible arrival of hundreds of new customers. Steiner started hand pumping the brine machine in the basement, while Parker called suppliers up and down the eastern seaboard to purchase more meat—large quantities of meat.

The line that Friday formed as Sheraton said it would. By noon, it snaked from in front of the deli on Seventh Avenue around the block to West 54th Street. Passing pedestrians thought it was some sort of free food giveaway or a movie or television audition.

The Carnegie Deli had hand cured double the usual amount, but by 3:00 P.M. it ran out of pastrami. In the future, it would never run out of cured meat again.

Steiner and Parker thought that the Friday customer blitz had been a one-day affair, much like extra business on St. Patrick's

Day. But on Saturday, lines formed again and continued to form days after. Deli-loving New Yorkers made a detour to eat at the Carnegie, sampled the cured meats, and agreed with Mimi Sheraton. The Carnegie Deli did serve the "Tops."

One review in New York's most important newspaper had launched the Carnegie Deli into the sky like the brightest of fireworks, and everyone in New York took notice. Everything good that happened afterward to the Carnegie Deli can be traced to this generous article.

1983: *Broadway Danny Rose*

Comedians loved Leo Steiner because he usually picked up the check. The Carnegie Deli became a hangout for Milton Berle, Henny Youngman, Jackie Mason, Joey Adams, Morey Amsterdam, and other Borscht Belt comedians. Steiner even joined the Friars Club, the fraternal organization of show business. He said, "Maybe I love comics because you need a big mouth to eat my sandwiches."

Woody Allen loved the Carnegie Deli and decided that it would make the perfect setting for scenes in his film *Broadway Danny Rose*. The restaurant closed for three days to allow the director time for shooting.

The film's story begins in the deli where a group of comedians (Corbett Monica, Sandy Baron, Jackie Gayle, and Will Jordan) swap anecdotes about showbiz legend Danny Rose. Rose is a big-hearted, no-luck agent who develops an empathetic bond with his no-talent performers.

Milton Berle, Sammy Davis Jr., and Leo Steiner, playing a counterman, had bit parts in the film. After the movie opened in 1984, more tourists started to come into the Carnegie Deli. The film had been terrific free advertising. Milton Parker thought the inside looked a little worn and repainted the interior, sprucing up the walls for the first renovation since 1937.

The movie is memorable for the description of one of Danny Rose's performers whose act featured a singing parrot. The bird closed the act by singing "I Gotta Be Me."

Parker said years later, "For $6,500—what Woody paid us for the three-day shoot—we received millions of dollars of free publicity."

1983: DELI WILLIAMSBURG BRIDGE

In May 1983, President Ronald Reagan welcomed the Summit of Industrialized Nations to Williamsburg, Virginia, including the heads of state from Japan, France, Germany, Italy, Great Britain, Canada, and the European Economic Community.

Although these heads of state brought disparate economic ideas to the conference, they had one surprising thing in common. This was the first and perhaps the only occasion when these dignitaries consumed New York-style delicatessen, with apparent relish.

At brunch time, into the mouths of Prime Minister Margaret Thatcher, Chancellor Helmut Kohl, President François Mitterrand, Prime Minister Yasuhiro Nakasone, Prime Minister Amitore Fanfani, and Prime Minister Pierre Trudeau popped lox and bagels, blueberry blintzes, and even pastrami.

Why? Because on this day in May, the official cuisine of the United States was delicatessen fare prepared by the Carnegie Deli's Leo Steiner. In a *New York Post* photograph of President Reagan congratulating the various U.S. chefs asked to prepare American meals, Steiner wears—perhaps for the only time in his life—the toque, the traditional tall white chef's cap.

An aide to Mayor Ed Koch recalled Steiner preparing the brunch for these eminent heads of state. He said, "For Jews, after 5,000 years of European suffering, this was our revenge."

Steiner, who had never heard a joke he couldn't try to top, said, "We can teach these Europeans what heartburn was all about."

1986: ONE ORDER, CASH TO GO

In the early morning hours of February 7, the Carnegie Deli experienced its most unusual takeout order: armed robbers wanted the cash.

The deli always stayed open until 4 A.M. and then reopened its doors at 6 A.M. The seven robbers must have canvassed the place or received an inside tip about the window of opportunity, because the holdup occurred at 4:45 A.M.

The thieves entered through a fire exit, surprising Sam Steiner, Leo's brother, two dishwashers, and a deliveryman.

A thug toting a sawed-off shotgun struck Steiner in the eye and ordered him and the staff on the floor "or we'll blow you away."

The robbers forced open the cash register and took the night's receipts. Then the gang fled into the deserted street. The robbers were never identified.

Sam Steiner refused medical treatment for a minor eye injury, preferring to visit his own physician.

But Leo Steiner had the last word. "The schmucks took the money and left the pastrami."

Less than three hours after the holdup, the Carnegie Deli opened for business. A new pickproof system was installed at the fire door.

In the best show business tradition, Steiner said, "The delicatessen and the show must go on."

1986: STATUE OF CHOPPED LIVER-TY

At the start of 1986, the nation anticipated plans for the celebration honoring the centennial of the Statue of Liberty, the wonderful gift from the people of France.

On July 4, Independence Day, President Ronald Reagan and other national and international dignitaries would honor the statue with speeches and fanfare.

October 25 marked the actual day for the one-hundredth anniversary. In attendance on that historic day in 1886 were President Grover Cleveland; the statue's French sculptor, Frederic-Auguste Bartholdi; and Joseph Pulitzer, whose *World* newspaper had raised the money from ordinary Americans to fund the pedestal.

It was also on that day in 1886 that office boys, working in Wall Street's brokerage houses, unraveled spools of tape and threw the streamers out of the window onto the crowd of 20,000 people assembled for the opening. The storm of white confetti that rained down marked the city's first ticker tape parade.

What could the Carnegie Deli do to celebrate the hundredth anniversary of this memorable event? Parker wanted to buy a small statue and surround it with chopped liver in the shape of Liberty Island. But Steiner believed that a fitting tribute to "The Lady" was to make a replica of the statue from 60 pounds of chopped liver. A wobbly version appeared in the deli's window. Carnegie Deli customers were treated to the first and only Statue of Liver-ty that tasted delicious.

1987: YES, VIRGINIA, THERE IS A CARNEGIE DELI

In October 1987, the Carnegie Deli opened a satellite restaurant in Tyson's Corner, Virginia—until then not an especially delicatessen-sounding place. It opened not in an old or refurbished building redolent with food aromas, but in the new Embassy Suite Hotel.

The staff had been imported from New York City, including waiters, counter people, the head cook, and, for the gala opening night festivities, Leo Steiner with that permanent Carnegie Deli Manhattan fixture, Henny Youngman.

The origin of this restaurant began with the first visit to the Carnegie Deli by Bruce Goldstein, a real estate magnate from Minneapolis who could not find pastrami worth eating while living in the Gopher State. After each business trip to Manhattan—and the customary stop at the Carnegie—he had visions of eating pastrami more often. How? By opening a Carnegie Deli in the Washington, DC, area.

Goldstein was not the first out-of-towner to be seduced by the notion of owning and operating a Carnegie Deli. New Yorkers who made the exodus to other parts of the United States always lamented, "There's no authentic New York deli where we live."

It took Goldstein years of persuading Steiner to make the deal, which included the real estate tycoon providing a half-million dollars of his own. The new deli opened with fanfare, gleaming white china, extra-large sandwiches, and hopes that 13 million square feet of adjoining office space would attract a deli food crowd.

It lasted for a few years. A Carnegie Deli regular in Manhattan predicted the outcome. "How can you duplicate this New York deli? Or the old ceiling? The old waiters? And Leo waltzing around? They'll be too polite in Tyson's Corner."

LEO STEINER, OWNER: "INTO THE DELI LIMELIGHT"

L eo Steiner answered the question of what it takes to run a successful delicatessen in a 1984 interview with restaurant/food critic Mimi Sheraton that appeared in *Manhattan, Inc.* magazine. He said, "You have to love food, but most of all you have to love people. Otherwise, go into another business. Customers are doing us a favor and deserve good food, fair value, and decent service."

The key to success in the restaurant trade is made up of three variables: location, quality, service. The Carnegie Deli is located just north of the theater district and in the heart of Manhattan's tourist hotel area. The deli needed a person with star quality to turn it into a celebrated, one-of-a-kind, New York hit. Leo Steiner proved to be that person, the man with delicatessen pizzazz.

Leo Steiner was the visible heart and soul of the Carnegie Deli from 1976 until his death on the last day of 1987. For 11 years, every newspaper, every magazine article, and every broadcast interview featured his voice or face. He emerged as the leading man in the Carnegie Deli's theatrical play, receiving great reviews. His partner Milton Parker was content to be the unnoticed, behind-the-scenes producer, working in the background, and leaving the public role to his extroverted partner.

Comedians adored Steiner, and they found a home away from home at the deli. He spoke the language of corny jokes— and corned beef and pastrami.

Steiner was born in 1939 in Elizabeth, New Jersey, of immigrant parents, and grew up speaking Yiddish and also English. He started his career in his midteens by working as a busboy in Zeigler's, a resort in upstate Sullivan County, New York.

The fluency in both languages proved to be the link that first led to an interest in the food business: At the resort, he translated the Yiddish of Mama Zeigler, the cook, to the non-Yiddish-speaking kitchen staff. Steiner was set to work slicing and dicing and doing other kitchen chores. He was most interested in the preparation of dishes and not in the cooking. He learned that success depended on finding the highest-quality ingredients.

He said, "It's hard to make suppliers understand you want the best, with no corners cut. A bakery sends me delicious Danish made with butter, and I'm pleased. Suddenly, three weeks later, they start using margarine in the mix."

Steiner also learned other valuable details at Zeigler's; customers loved large portions that spilled over their plate, and it helped to have a good sense of humor and some common-sense smarts, called *seichel* in Yiddish.

Steiner found work in a small Manhattan luncheonette, and then partnered with Ray Weiss in Pastrami 'n Things on East 23rd Street. Over time, he developed a method for hand curing pastrami and corned beef. He experimented with different ingredients to achieve the perfect meat coating, and he insisted that the curing be done by the old method from a hand-pumped brine machine.

Taking Over the Carnegie

When restaurant brokers and future silent partners Freddie Klein, Sidney Small, and Bill Landesman (Parker's brother-in-law) searched for a team to take over the Carnegie Deli, they realized they needed a front man with food skills and an office man who could watch costs and handle scheduling. The new team was Leo Steiner and Milton Parker, one of the most successful blind date marriages in restaurant history.

In their first meeting, Parker admitted to Steiner that he had never operated a sit-down delicatessen. Parker said, "I'm a businessman."

"Don't worry, Milton," said Steiner with customary good cheer. "I'll carry you until you learn the deli business."

Steiner mentioned from the outset that the way the Carnegie Deli could succeed was to offer a better-tasting, higher-quality meal than the more famous Stage Delicatessen down the street. Parker agreed; he would assist Steiner in whatever it took to turn the Carnegie around, to make it into a top-flight delicatessen.

It took a few months for the former patrons from the area and a few musicians from Carnegie Hall to see whether the renovations were real or cosmetic. The returning diners were delighted with the improved taste of the pastrami and corned beef. There was lots of praise also for the free sour pickles and sour tomatoes on the tables.

In addition to becoming acquainted with the new and delicious taste of hand-cured meats, the old and new patrons met Leo Steiner, the ebullient co-owner who worked the floor. He chatted with everyone, and on occasion bought a free slice of cheesecake or apple strudel for a familiar face or for a customer from out of town.

A partnership rises and falls on trust, and when Steiner decided to enlarge the sandwiches by adding on more meat, Parker trusted that this attention grabber would succeed.

THE ARNOLD'S BREAD COMMERCIAL

The Carnegie Deli hired Herb Schlein, an actor, to be the deli's greeter and host. Schlein was well known by showbiz people and appeared in theatrical plays and local television shows. When he learned that the advertising agency for Arnold's Bread, a local bakery, was looking for an authentic-looking delicatessen person, he suggested that they stop by the Carnegie to interview him, Steiner, and Parker. The agency's art director videotaped a short segment of the three men and showed the clips to the client.

At first, Arnold's Bread and the ad agency wanted Parker because he was jovial and his pronunciation was impeccable. But the day of the shoot was Parker's one day off, and the pay of $90 did not seem worthwhile. He suggested Steiner as the replacement.

Steiner was delighted to do the television spot and appeared as the counterman making sandwiches with his distinctive New York accent saying, "It makes a nice sandwich . . . a nice sandwich." Years later, people continued to recognize him from the Arnold's commercial. What no one realized then was the future value of advertising residuals, monies paid for subsequent uses of the commercial: Steiner collected $50,000.

The menus represented the one noticeable change that came from Steiner's new showbiz celebrity. The Carnegie changed the menus to resemble a theater marquee with klieg light symbols.

"Plain and Simply Wonderful"

In March 1979, Mimi Sheraton penned her *New York Times* newspaper review that rated the Carnegie Deli the "Tops" in pastrami and corned beef preparation and taste. The highest accolade in New York City, this was an honor it shared with two area delis. Sheraton was effusive in her praise when she wrote, "The generous sandwiches of both corned beef and pastrami are plain and simply wonderful."

In the *Manhattan, Inc.* article, Steiner narrated in great detail about the hand-curing and serving method for making the pastrami. He also voiced an interesting opinion about cured meat sandwich eaters when he said, "The most serious deli customers are those who come in and have a corned beef or pastrami sandwich for dinner. Having deli for lunch is just a social grace."

Two years later, Sheraton would return incognito to write about New York blintzes, also handing the Carnegie Deli a top rating. The deli's blintz business increased a hundredfold. When PBS television food show host Burt Wolf reported about the blintzes, 10,000 people wrote to the Carnegie for the recipe.

Have a Nice Sandwich

In the following years, a number of events transpired in Leo Steiner's personal and professional life: He lost 60 pounds and married for the first time to Irma Birnbaum, a steady Carnegie customer.

He created a comedian's table for the comics to exchange shtick with him and with each other (much like the bantering in the opening of *Broadway Danny Rose*). He decided that if a classy restaurant like the 21 Club reserved an area of its dining room for "special" patrons, he would create a certain cachet with loyal celebrity customers by handing out linen napkins to the chosen few. (Ordinary diners used paper napkins.)

Abe Rosenthal, the legendary czar of the *New York Times*, was one of the deli-eating elite who was awarded the prestigious Leo Steiner linen napkin. He told Mimi Sheraton that it was one of the more treasured tributes he had ever received.

Jack Sirota, the Carnegie's waiter since 1959, observed Steiner over the years. He called the owner a "fabulous talker, a schmoozer with the customers." Steiner would talk to anyone and then flag down a server, point to the table, and say, "Bring this table some blintzes." Or "Bring a piece of cheesecake to these folks from out of town." The customers delighted in the free food and told friends about Steiner's generosity.

Food critic Mimi Sheraton became a good friend and a big booster. She judged Steiner by the same high standards as the owner of Lutèce, André Soltner. In 1984, she introduced these two disparate food experts as they talked with passion about restaurant life and sampled each other's cuisine. (Sheraton retired in 1983 as the *Times'* restaurant critic. Her most recent book is *Eating My Words, An Appetite for Life,* published in 2004 by William Morrow.)

That March 1979 bravura review turned Leo Steiner and the Carnegie Deli into bona fide New York celebrities. Steiner had achieved virtuoso status as the master worker of cured meats. His pastrami opus achieved the highest gustatory praise in the deli world. He even appeared on *Hollywood Squares.*

Steiner's first-rate sense of humor lent itself to amusing quotes and humorous interviews. Mimi Sheraton remembered that when Leo and Irma returned from their honeymoon in the south of France, he said how difficult it was to drive on the winding, curvy roads of the "Grand Knish" (Corniche).

Yet, even with the fame and celebrity, he wore a simple white apron and treated celebrities and everyday people with the same shticky hello. He handed out free slices of pastrami to people waiting in line. He often pointed to a table and instructed the server to add more meat to the sandwich.

He also loved New York City and criticized comments that deli was better in California. He said, "The salamis out in California are lousy. You know why? Because the water is lousy." When snooty customers demanded a "lean pastrami sandwich," Leo replied, "If you want lean pastrami, order the turkey breast."

EXPANSION

During this decade of the 1980s, investors tried to convince the two owners to open other branches of the by now famous Carnegie Deli throughout the United States. On paper, these offers (time and again with the ready availability of large sums of money) seemed like surefire moneymaking enterprises. Who would not want to eat Carnegie Deli pastrami or corned beef in every city in the United States?

Steiner envisioned that the Carnegie's reputation would spread throughout America, if the branch operations ordered the high-quality hand-cured meats and cheesecake from the Carnegie. He was eager to take the tasty menu and spread the cured meat joy to expatriate New Yorkers living in other cities. He was looking for new diners to charm.

EXIT LEO

On December 31, 1987, Leo Steiner, the ebullient, food-loving perfectionist and *mensch*, died of a brain tumor. The light of the deli world had been extinguished, and New York would not see his kind again.

In his final days, Steiner never lost his sense of humor or his timing. Commenting on the delicate brain surgery, he said,

"I'm afraid the doctors stole my recipes." In the hospital, he ordered sandwiches for the nurses and yelled at the deliveryman for forgetting the mustard and the pickles.

Steiner's funeral service took place at the Sutton Place Synagogue in Manhattan. A who's who of show business celebrities joined 700 other people for the funeral. The famous included Jerry Stiller, Henny Youngman, singers Mary Travers and Julius La Rosa, opera star Robert Merrill, and Joel Siegel from *Good Morning America*, and many CBS executives.

Henny Youngman and a lineup of comedians gave humorous eulogies of the man with the "rye" humor. Screenwriter Andrew Bergman (*The In-Laws*), describing the delicatessen's overstuffed sandwiches, said they were "meals that clog the arteries of a buffalo." A few one-liners came from Steiner on videotape, quipping, "Whaddaya mean is chicken soup good for you? Have you ever seen a chicken with a cold?"

That evening, hundreds of New York regulars gathered at the deli to celebrate Steiner's life by having a meal at the restaurant. One customer summed up the life of the deli man by saying, "Leo was like chicken fat. He had substance."

At the service, Henny Youngman dubbed his good friend "The Deli Lama." Warner Wolf, the sports anchor at WCBS, said, "If God needs an official greeter in heaven, he has a new one." Rabbi David Kahane spoke the last words, "More than the Prince of Pastrami, but also the Prince of People."

Leo Steiner, the hardworking food maven, the front man beloved by show business folk, was gone. The reputation for quality, however, that he had insisted upon from that first day in 1976 would survive and flourish years after him.

People would remember the first time he was quoted in Mimi Sheraton's 1979 article when he said, "What I like to hear is a customer saying: 'You make a nice sandwich. A nice sandwich.'"

THE DELI FOOD QUIZ

1. What is a knish?
   a. Pita bread pockets with chopped liver and chicken fat.
   b. Pastry filled with mashed potatoes or ground meat, and onions.
   c. Bialy layered with minced tongue, basil, and coriander.
   d. Phyllo dough filled with baked tripe and eggplant.

2. What other ethnic food is similar to kreplach?
   a. Wonton soup.
   b. Bauernwurst.
   c. Buffalo mozzarella in brodo.
   d. Haggis strips.

3. What ingredients go into a traditional chocolate egg cream?
   a. Eggs, Ovaltine, and cream soda.
   b. Yolk of an egg, Hershey's syrup, and tap water.
   c. Nonfat milk, carob powder, and bottled water.
   d. U-Bet syrup, iced whole milk, and seltzer.

4. What is kasha?
   a. Buckwheat groats.
   b. Latvian flat bread.
   c. Potato skin dumplings.
   d. Gooseneck liverwurst.

5. What is flanken?
   a. Pickled cows feet au gratin.
   b. Short ribs boiled.
   c. Roasted gizzards, garlic, and paprika.
   d. Sheep livers sautéed with shallots.

6. What's the doctor's name of Cel-Ray tonic fame?
   a. Dr. Askenase.
   b. Dr. Ettinger.
   c. Dr. Brown.
   d. Dr. Holt.

(continued)

THE DELI FOOD QUIZ (CONTINUED)

7. What is rugelach?
   a. Star-shaped marzipan candy served during Passover.
   b. Crescent-shaped pastry filled with raisins or dried fruit.
   c. Oval-shaped tartlets with almonds and mocha cream.
   d. Balls of honeyed dough rolled in confectioners' sugar.

8. Gefilte fish is made from what kind of fish?
   a. Atlantic flounder.
   b. Prince Lewis cod.
   c. Whitefish or carp.
   d. White Cloud Mountain fish.

9. What best describes derma (beef casing with matzoh meal, onion, and suet)?
   a. Stuffed.
   b. Kishkaed.
   c. Crammed.
   d. Crowded.

10. What is usually served on top of a blintz?
    a. Salsa piquant or hot pepper sauce.
    b. Spinach-leek purée.
    c. Loganberry mayonnaise.
    d. Sour cream.

Scoring:

9 to 10:   You are a connoisseur of deli food.
5 to 8:   You have some tasty deli experiences in your past.
Below 5:   You need to make more trips to your nearest deli.

Answers: 1b, 2a, 3d, 4a, 5b, 6c, 7b, 8c, 9a, 10d

The writer Andrew Bergman summed up Leo Steiner's happy life by saying, "He made you feel like he had waited all day to see you."

APPETIZERS, SIDE DISHES, AND SAUCES

Tasty, distinctive appetizers mark the history of New York delicatessen food. These are wonderful morsels to have before a deli meal. And there are also some interesting deli side dishes and sauces.

Herring

Historically, the little herring has been the fish of the common folk, the poor man's food. From Finland to Portugal, the fish found its way to Europe's tables either served fresh or, more commonly, salted.

The reason for the fish's popularity was its low price. Taking the herring in plentiful supply from the cold seas in large nets, fishermen could bring back large quantities, which local merchants salted or pickled or sold fresh to the better-paying customers.

In Scandinavia, herring is the national dish, served more often and in greater variety than any other fish or any meat. On April Fool's Day in Sweden, the people say, "April, you are a dumb herring that I can fool all the time."

In Holland, another herring-loving country, the saying goes, "If there's herring here, the doctor is far away." A treat is to eat herring with bread or toast in many of the Netherlands' outdoor food markets.

Eastern Europeans became herring merchants, importing the fish by railway from Holland and Baltic Sea countries into Poland, Russia, and Germany. From the distributors, the fish was sold to fishmongers, food stores, and also to the nomadic herring peddlers who visited the *shtetls* with their pushcarts.

The tasty herring was vital to the diet of the population living so far from the sea. Often, the fish represented the only protein available. In the 1920s, Polish Jews were reported to have eaten a herring a day.

Delicatessen customers recognize two different types of herring, the *schmaltz* and the *matjes*. *Schmaltz* herring is made with kosher or coarse salt. Then, the salted fish are left to stand in barrels for three to five days. *Matjes* is fresh herring preserved in a brine solution for about one hour. In the Netherlands, the *matjes* is sometimes soaked in milk for a delicate flavor.

The versatile herring can be eaten in many different ways. After it is filleted and skinned, it can be served with sour cream and onions or eaten fresh with olive oil and lemon. Many prefer herring in light vinegar or wine solution.

Matzoh Ball

In Exodus 12:8, God says, "And they shall eat the flesh in that night, roast with fire, and unleavened bread; and with bitter herbs they shall eat it." The bread (or matzoh) became known as the bread of affliction, representing the departure from Egypt.

There was no time to bake leavened bread, so the fleeing masses had to eat the crackerlike bread with its bland taste. If matzohs are made at home, Jewish custom requires that they must be baked in 18 minutes or less.

The Bible says that the Israelites, fleeing the wicked Egyptian Pharaoh, wandered in the desert for 40 years, and in that time many must have realized that the taste of matzoh was as dry as the sands of the desert.

Matzoh continued as part of the Passover tradition for ages. But somewhere in Eastern Europe an Ashkenazi Jewish cook took the meal that makes matzoh, rolled it into a ball, and dropped it into boiling water to cook it. What to do with this ball? Maybe serve it up in a nice chicken stock soup.

When Eastern European Jews immigrated to the United States in great numbers after 1880, settling along the eastern seaboard, they relied on small, local bakeries for matzoh. In 1883, the Horowitz family opened the first commercial bakery in New York City to supply matzohs for the burgeoning, newly arrived population.

Those who complain about the transformation of the traditional bagel into new varieties with raisins, sun-dried tomatoes, or other aberrations should look at what has happened to matzoh. In all other months before and after Passover, to make matzoh more palatable as a year-round food, the large matzoh bakeries have brought out boxes of salted, egg and onion, and the most egregious variety: chocolate-covered matzoh.

Matzoh ball soup is graded on the Grandma Glassberg Scale of Viscosity; if the spoon can stand upright in the broth, it is thick enough. The Carnegie Deli serves up a delicious soup, and if you want to make this dish, the recipe is found on page 38.

Coleslaw

This universal deli side dish is the unheralded chorus line that backs up the sandwich stars. No one praises the coleslaw in a deli, but if it is not to your taste, it is the first food to draw complaints.

Coleslaw is cabbage shredded with a few other vegetables, and mixed primarily with vinegar and mayonnaise. The varieties of this side dish are boundless; the recipes come from all cultures.

The term derives from the Dutch term *kool sla*, translated as "cabbage salad." Food historians believe that the original *kool sla* made in Holland was served hot.

Mayonnaise

Homemade coleslaw in America owes a debt of thanks to Richard Hellmann. By 1912, he started marketing bottled mayonnaise in the United States under his own name.

And mayonnaise owes its existence to France's duc de Richelieu, who in 1756 defeated the British forces at Port Mahon. To commemorate the triumph, the duke's chef prepared a victory feast sauce. Lacking fresh cream, the chef substituted olive oil to mix in with the eggs. The light, creamy sauce was a big hit, and the chef named it after his patron's victory, "Mahonnaise."

Russian Dressing

The most popular deli sandwich dressing comes from Russia, where it was made with mayonnaise, a thick tomato sauce, chives, pimentos, spices, and caviar.

In the United States, the dressing is usually made using 1 cup mayonnaise, 1 cup Heinz Tomato Ketchup, 2 tablespoons India or hamburger relish, salt, and a little sugar. Some people add a dash of Worcestershire sauce.

Food trivia: The reason for the slogan Heinz 57 Varieties is that H. J. Heinz, the company's founder, liked the way the number sounded even though the Pittsburgh-based company made many more than 57 food products. Later, the H. J. Heinz Company offered Joe DiMaggio $25,000 if his 1941 consecutive games hitting streak reached the company's well-advertised 57. Unhappily for the Yankee Clipper, the streak ended at 56.

Mustard

When New Yorkers speak of "deli mustard," they mean darkish brown, khaki-colored mustard with a robust flavor. They never place yellow mustard in this deli class; the latter is often associated with the Midwest and served in that section of the country's Major League baseball stadiums.

Mustard has been around for a long time, and the French are credited with making it palatable, most memorably by the House of Maille founded in 1747. Later, mustard making would shift to the southern city of Dijon. Colman's distinct English mustard was first sold in 1804.

In the United States, the Germans introduced their own brand of mustard in the nation's first delicatessens. Gulden's was founded in 1862, and its now familiar-shaped jar advertises "Spicy Brown Mustard" on the label, a secret recipe for 142 years.

The darkish brown mustard complements perfectly the spicy cured meats, especially tongue sandwiches.

The K Foods: Kreplach, Knish, and Kasha

Kreplach are soup dumplings originally made from leftover meat, but they can be equally good made from freshly prepared ground beef. The noodle dough is rich and soft, and not too difficult to make. See the Carnegie Deli's recipe for kreplach on page 39.

Knishes are Old World pastry, consisting of thick dough filled with mashed potatoes, onions, kasha, or ground meat. The versatile knish can be served as a side dish or as an appetizer.

The one name married to the knish is Yonah Schimmel; a store bearing this name still makes and sells fresh knishes in the same handmade manner on Houston Street in New York. The tradition has continued since 1910.

In Poland and Russia, *kasha* refers to any cooked grains like millet or buckwheat. In the United States, kasha is exclusively buckwheat groats.

The appeal of kasha is its distinctive nutty and toasty flavor, which blends in with noodles and vegetables.

Try the Carnegie Deli's kasha varnishkas recipe on page 36.

APPETIZER AND SIDE DISH RECIPES

CHOPPED LIVER
(Makes Enough for Ten Servings)

Chopped liver is one of the traditional appetizer delights found only in a delicatessen. It can be a sandwich by itself, a combo sandwich with other meats, or served as a salad with lettuce, tomato, and onion.

Ingredients

1 pound chicken livers
½ cup olive oil
½ cup water
1 medium green onion, chopped
3 eggs, hard-boiled and chopped
Sugar, salt, and pepper to taste

Instructions

1. Bake the chicken livers in the oil and water in a roasting pan at 450 degrees for 1½ hours.
2. Cook the onion in a separate pan until it is soft.
3. Remove livers and dry on a paper towel to absorb the oil.
4. In a grinder (or with a fine chopper), chop the livers, onions, and eggs until very fine.
5. Add sugar, salt, and pepper to taste.
6. Mix well.
7. Refrigerate until use.

To Serve

In addition to sandwiches and salads, chopped liver makes a nice premeal or snack dip. Try serving with small slices of pumpernickel or dark brown bread.

Kasha Varnishkas
(Serves Six)

This tasty side dish or appetizer has a distinct taste that says "delicatessen." It's easy to make and will allow you to say—for the only time in your life—the words "buckwheat groats."

Ingredients

1 box bow-tie noodles (farfalle)
1 medium green onion, chopped
1 tablespoon olive oil
1 cup kasha (buckwheat groats). These can be purchased in the international aisle of a supermarket, the kosher section, or online.
2 cups chicken stock
Salt and pepper to taste

Instructions

1. Cook the noodles according to the directions on the box.
2. Cook the onion in the olive oil until soft.
3. Mix the kasha and the onion until the kasha kernels pull apart.
4. Add stock and simmer for 15 minutes.
5. Blend cooked kasha with the noodles.
6. Add salt and pepper to taste.

To Serve

This is best served in a pasta bowl, which optimizes the spoonfuls of kasha, onions, and noodles. This dish is also excellent as a leftover and can be easily rewarmed.

BARLEY SOUP
(Serves Four)

This soup that Mama used to make will put marrow in your bones.

Ingredients

1 pound flanken (plate brisket)
1 marrowbone
2 quarts water
½ cup pearl barley
2 white onions, diced
2 carrots, diced
Salt and pepper to taste

Instructions

1. Cover meat and marrowbone with salted water and bring to a boil.
2. Reduce heat and simmer for an hour.
3. Wash and drain barley.
4. Add barley and vegetables to stock.
5. Simmer until barley is tender (about 1½ hours).
6. Season to taste.

To Serve

For family meals, this soup is usually served in a large tureen and ladled out. Encourage sucking the delicious marrow from the bone.

MATZOH BALL SOUP
(Serves Twenty)

This classic matzoh ball soup recipe remains a favorite at the Carnegie Deli. The matzoh balls are large and flavorful and the broth is rich. Perfect for a chilly day or, for that matter, any day.

Ingredients

30 eggs
2⅓ cups liquid shortening or olive oil
2 cups water
5 pounds matzoh meal
Salt and pepper to taste
Consommé (see page 118)

Instructions

1. In a large bowl, mix the eggs, shortening, water, matzoh meal, and seasoning. The mixture should be thick but manageable. Place it in the refrigerator to chill. This makes it easier to handle.
2. By hand, form round balls about the size of a billiard ball.
3. Boil the balls for 45 minutes in consommé (see page 118).

To Serve

Serve two matzoh balls per portion.

Kreplach with Meat
(Makes Thirty Servings)

These dumplings are a delicious adjunct to any meat dish. They are made during Jewish holidays, but are good any time of the year.

Ingredients for Dough

2 eggs
½ teaspoon salt
1 tablespoon warm water
1 cup flour

Instructions for Making Dough

1. In a large mixing bowl, mix the flour, salt, eggs, and water until the dough is smooth.
2. Roll out the dough and slice it into 8 pieces.
3. On a board covered with flour, roll out each of the 8 pieces until they are ⅛-inch thick and cut out about 4 circles (approximately 3 inches in diameter) from each piece.

Ingredients for Filling

½ pound chopped ground beef (use lean meat such as ground round)
1 small green onion, chopped
1 egg
Salt and pepper to taste

Instructions for Making Filling

1. Sauté the ground meat and the onion until the meat is brown and then mix in the egg, salt, and pepper.
2. Place ½ teaspoon of the meat mixture into each dough circle. Fold in half and pinch edges tight to seal. Then pull the edges of the half circle back and pinch to form a triangle. Continue until all the pressed kreplach are made.
3. Drop the kreplach into boiling water to cook for 15 minutes.

To Serve

Serve these dumplings with brisket or roast chicken.

KNISH
(Makes Two Pieces)

The knish is a staple and inexpensive delicacy. The unwritten rules for what makes a true knish are: It is baked (never fried), always handmade, and filled with potatoes or vegetables.

Ingredients

6 medium-sized potatoes
⅓ cup onions, minced
2 tablespoons olive oil
2 tablespoons chicken broth
Salt and pepper to taste
6 sheets of phyllo dough (available in the frozen food section)

Instructions

1. Peel the potatoes and cut in half.
2. Boil the potatoes in salted water until tender, then mash.
3. Sauté the onions in olive oil.
4. Mix the mashed potatoes, onions, broth, salt, and pepper.
5. Heat the oven to 375 degrees.
6. Cut the stack of phyllo dough in half.
7. Spoon 1 cup of the potato/onion mixture into each part of the dough.
8. Mold the dough around the filling into medium-sized balls, pinching the ends closed.
9. Prick the tops lightly with a toothpick.
10. Place dough on a baking sheet or pan and brush lightly with butter or oil.
11. Bake for 30 to 35 minutes until the knishes turn golden brown.

To Serve

Knishes can be eaten as a snack or with meats as a side dish.

With Love from CARNEGIE DELICATESSEN & RESTAURANT

HENNY YOUNGMAN: KING OF THE ONE-LINERS

Henny Youngman was the one comedian most associated with the Carnegie Deli. The deli was his private clubhouse after he returned from doing one-night stands in the heartland and also after he retired permanently from show business. He lived close by in an apartment near Fifth Avenue and West 55th Street.

Youngman was frequently seen at his usual Carnegie Deli table eating Henny's Heaven, a sandwich named after him (lox, cream cheese, and a Bermuda onion on a bagel). Henny came in so often that he knew the names of the servers, the cooks, and the countermen. He palled around with Leo Steiner and was influential in nominating the Carnegie's owner for membership in the Friars Club.

HENNY: "The horse I bet on was so slow, the jockey kept a diary of the race."

Henny accompanied Steiner for the opening of the Tyson's Corner restaurant. He gave the eulogy at Steiner's poignant memorial; his photograph appeared in the New York newspapers, greeting Steiner's widow.

HENNY: "A man goes to a psychiatrist. The doctor says, 'You're crazy.' The man says, 'I want a second opinion.' The doctor replies, 'You're ugly, too.'"

Youngman's career spanned seven decades. He began as a violin-playing bandleader of the Sewanee Syncopaters in the 1920s in the Catskill Mountains. In those days, the bandleader did the talking and Youngman's funny warm-up chatter with the audience proved more interesting than the band.

HENNY: "My agent called me, asking, 'How much to do a movie with Farrah Fawcett? How about $20,000?' I said, 'I'll pay it.'"

It was during his appearance on singer Kate Smith's radio show in 1937 that audiences first heard his trademark remark, "Take my wife, please." It was a joke that continued for the happily married comic until his wife died in 1987 and it was also the title of his 1973 autobiography. For the radio show, Youngman used many comic writers, some of whom became famous years later, like Buddy Hackett, Jack Carter, and Red Buttons.

Youngman's staccato one-liners used a rim-shot delivery style that succeeded best in front of a live audience. He toured the country, appearing as many as 200 times a year in big-city and small-town nightclubs. In the 1960s, his career received a boost when his style proved ideal for the joke-rich *Laugh-In* television program. College students rediscovered the master of the one-liners.

HENNY TO HECKLER: "If you have your life to live over again, don't do it."

The short, punchy delivery was also the perfect format for the Dial-A-Joke service offered in 1974 by the New York telephone company. He attracted as many as three million calls a month, offering a rapid six jokes in a minute.

HENNY: "She's been married so many times, she has rice marks on her face."

After his wife Sadie died, the Carnegie Deli became Youngman's second home. When he stopped touring at age 85, he was in the delicatessen daily, exchanging barbed remarks with the servers.

Youngman's frugality was the stuff of legend. One comic said of him, if he could wash off used toothpaste, he would squeeze it back into the tube. Youngman asked longtime Carnegie Deli waiter Jack Sirota—whom he first met in 1959—"Jack, tell the truth. Am I a good tipper?" Sirota replied, "Henny, you're a great tipper . . . if it was still 1935."

HENNY: "You have the Midas touch. Everything you touch turns into a muffler."

When Henny died in 1998 at age 91, the media came to the Carnegie Deli for Henny Youngman anecdotes from the owner and the staff. The media knew that for 50 years or more, Henny could be found in the Carnegie Deli, enjoying the delicatessen, kibitzing with customers, and eating a Henny's Heaven sandwich.

HENNY: "To my nephew Irving, who has pestered me forever to mention him in my will, I oblige: 'Hello, Irving.'"

Wayne Lammers, Waiter: "The Deli Music Man"

Pedestrians passing by the Carnegie Deli or customers waiting in line in front of the deli notice a small television set in the window below the hanging salamis. It plays over and over again what is billed as "the world's greatest deli musical," a brilliantly hilarious, 17-minute cinematic tribute to the food and staff.

Wayne Lammers is the star of the show, the lyricist (Pete Levin wrote the music), and the co-director (along with Henry Chalfont) of this delightful film extravaganza. Lammers is a regular Carnegie waiter and a talented working performer with 23 comic music videos to his credit.

The origin of the musical is that management, Milton Parker and Sandy Levine, wanted to offer some entertainment to the customers waiting in line. They asked their one authentic show-biz waiter for his ideas for an original video production. This free-ranging concept was music to Lammers' ears because he had been thinking for years about a parody of life at the Carnegie.

Lammers realized that for the musical to succeed it needed "rye" lyrics, catchy music, and Busby Berkeley–type musical numbers with the entire staff participating. The owners responded warmly to the lyrics, financed the production, and allowed the camera crew into the deli for the shoot.

To date, thousands of people have seen the video, which also plays in the Carnegie's back dining room. It has been shown at the Smithsonian and was sent to a film festival about food in Italy. Lammers believes it should be shown at the Sundance Film Festival. A copy can be purchased for $15.00 at the deli counter.

Lammers has been a waiter at the Carnegie for seven years. Like other performers committed to show business, his career has witnessed its ups and downs. He's worked at New York's Public Theatre and written a political rhyming Dr. Seuss-type musical that *The New Yorker* review said "cast a wry, satiric eye on American culture past and present."

Taking pride in being a professional waiter, Lammers adheres to Noel Coward's advice about dealing with people that comes from the musical *Sail Away*: "Pander to him morning, noon, and night. The customer's always right."

Lammers' most memorable Carnegie Deli show business story occurred when a famous actor (no names, please) spotted his ex-wife's photograph hanging on the Deli Wall of Fame. The marital split had been acrimonious and quite public, and when the man saw his ex-wife, he saw red. First he badmouthed his former spouse and then, enraged, smashed her picture to pieces.

A permanent part of the waitstaff, Lammers continues to write more creative shows.

Customers of the Carnegie Deli

To bring back memories of your visit to the Carnegie, go online to www.PeteLevin.com/carnegie.htm to view the familiar staff and learn the history of the deli musical. Also take a look at talented Pete Levin's musical biography.

MILTON PARKER, OWNER: "HARD WORK AND GOOD LUCK"

Milton Parker's main goal in life was to provide a good living for his wife and children. His plan was straightforward: to work hard and to save money by counting pennies. Because he was born in 1919 and grew up during the Depression years of the 1930s, he always wanted to be in business for himself. Knowing he could not work a nine-to-five job for any company, he never had pipe dreams of celebrity, riches, and fame.

By 1950, after trying a few sales jobs, he had saved enough money to own a small luncheonette, a location that he worked with his brother-in-law, Milton Levy. To avoid confusion, Levy was called Milton and Parker was called Parker.

The store was on East Broadway and Rutgers Street in New York City. The men had no experience in the retail trade and had to learn how to make sandwiches and egg creams. The profit, what there was of it, came in pennies and nickels. Kids stealing candy and gum cut into the margin. Four years and many petty robberies later, they handed back the store. Working seven days a week and 18 hours a day had not proved successful.

Then, the brothers-in-law bought an open-window lunch-eonette on Lafayette and Spring Streets in SoHo (*South of Houston* Street), Manhattan. These open-window stores were common in New York City; sandwiches were made in the rear and sold to customers for takeout or to eat at the few seats inside the luncheonette.

They worked this location for four years until 1958. Making a small profit, the men moved to another luncheonette at Avenue Z and Ocean Parkway in Brooklyn in a development known as Beach Haven and owned by Fred Trump. Parker remembered that Donald Trump's mother arrived in a chauffeured limousine, wearing a fur coat, to collect the dimes from the family-owned washing machine concessions.

After seven years toiling in the backwaters of Brooklyn, the team headed out to Long Island, finding a promising spot in Levittown where they opened a luncheonette and ice-cream parlor in a new shopping center. The hope was that this upscale location, which included May's Department Store, a Grand Union Supermarket, and a Singer Sewing Center, would generate sufficient traffic to be the last stop for the wandering owners. Levy died and Parker took in another partner.

After 12 years, the shopping center had changed for the worse, as had the business. Parker looked at the diminishing revenues and realized there was not enough income in the Long Island location for two men with families. He gave up his half of the store to the new partner.

What to do next? Parker was 56 and had worked long hours for more than 25 years, selling sodas, sandwiches, gift cards, and magazines. His work ethic and the ability to concentrate on the bottom line had come to the attention of another brother-in-law, Bill Landesman, a partner in a restaurant brokerage business in Manhattan. He suggested Parker as a potential partner for food maven Leo Steiner to take over the Carnegie Deli. In addition, the brokers brought in Abe Shtulman as a partner.

Leo Meets Milton

Parker remembered the first time he met Steiner, who in those days was a roly-poly 200 pounds, someone who loved to eat the food he prepared. Parker's prior food experience had been limited to sandwich making; he had no hot food knowledge. In Steiner, Parker recognized a person who knew food. Parker paid Steiner the ultimate tribute by calling him "a real deli man."

On visits to the deli, Parker witnessed apathy among the waitstaff; they seemed to know the delicatessen was up for sale. He also canvassed the deli from top to bottom, noticing a workplace that needed a good cleaning and a paint job.

The negotiations to sell the deli lasted through the night. The deal was signed. Five people—Parker, Steiner, and Mark Shtulman (Abe's son) and the two silent partners, Abe Shtulman and Ray Weiss—would each own 20 percent of the Carnegie Deli.

Parker studied the layout of the dining room. He calculated that if he cut the tables down by two inches and rearranged them in the same-sized space, he could increase the number of seats from 92 to 122, a net gain of 25 percent.

Pressing the Partnership

Parker's first surprise occurred when he noticed that Steiner had set out on each table a bowl of free handmade sour pickles and sour tomatoes. The second shock came when he witnessed Steiner enlarge the size of the meat sandwiches to a height never before seen in a Manhattan deli.

Parker protested and said, "Leo, we're not going to make any money on these sandwiches unless we raise prices."

Steiner replied, "Give me two or three months with the big sandwiches at the regular price."

Parker noticed that Dave, the counterman, responded to Steiner's carte blanche for larger sandwiches by piling on meat to every order he prepared. Parker lamented, "Dave, please, you're killing me." But Dave continued following Steiner's order.

Two years later, in January 1979, business was fair. Steiner and Parker bought out Weiss' and the two Shtulmans' shares. They sold 20 percent to the restaurant brokers, and the two working partners ended up with 40 percent each.

Business started to improve after Mimi Sheraton's *New York Times* review in March 1979. The lines started to form for a taste of New York City's best-rated pastrami. Parker was surprised also to hear people in line say, "This is the place. This is the place with the big sandwiches."

The partnership evolved into a Mr. Inside (Parker) and Mr. Outside (Steiner). Parker was content to remain out of sight in the back office. He shared none of Steiner's desire to become a public figure, recognized by customers or show business people. It was not a case that Parker lacked the personality; he had a dry wit, but he realized that Steiner possessed a natural bent for schmoozing. And he knew that the spotlight would shine brighter on the one Carnegie Deli person in the limelight.

Parker gave the credit to his partner for being the publicity person whose persona and shtick was the face of the Carnegie Deli. Steiner ordered the food, supervised its preparation, and judged if the cooking and serving met his standards. Parker stated that he "was the guy who made sure the payroll went out on time, oversaw the cleaning of the restaurant, and picked up the papers on the floor."

For 11 years, no one had seen a picture of Milton Parker in a newspaper or magazine article. No one had asked Parker for an interview about the food, the food preparation, or any of the deli's promotions.

PARKER PENS HIS OWN NAME

In January 1988, after Steiner's funeral, Parker took center stage. He was confident that business would not decline after his partner's death; most customers came for a delicious delicatessen meal. Maybe the comedians would feel the personal loss of their soulmate and Friars Club pal.

In May 1988, five months after Steiner's death, a picture of Milton Parker appeared in a full-color page in the magazine, *Manhattan, Inc.* The headline trumpeted: "New Carnegie King Carries a Big Shtick." The subheadline informed the public that someone else was in charge of the Carnegie Deli: "Partner Parker Packs the Pickles Now That the Pastrami King Has Passed On."

For a curious public and for the deli regulars, the photograph was a jolt. The delicatessen man in the photo wore the shirt and tie of a businessman and not the white apron of a cook, which Steiner had always worn. Parker carried on his shoulder a four-foot, giant replica of a pickle.

Parker, the pragmatist, responded in blunt terms to the canonization of Leo Steiner, the actions by Bruce Goldstein, who had opened and funded the Tyson's Corner Carnegie Deli branch. Goldstein, unhappy that the deli food maven had died, put Leo Steiner's life story on the back of the Virginia Carnegie Deli menus. He also wanted to have celebrated caricaturist, Al Hirschfeld, do a likeness of Steiner for the menu.

Milton said, "When someone dies, I don't think it's right to keep bringing him up." And he added, "I miss Leo, and I'd like to have him sitting here at the deli instead of me. I'd be in Aruba." It was a funny line and one Steiner would have appreciated.

At age 69, when other businessmen typically retire, Milton Parker returned to the center ring and became the sole impresario of the Carnegie Deli.

Handling the Deli Crowd

CBS boss William Paley and former Secretary of State Henry Kissinger (two linen napkins on their laps) and their wives came in for dinner. Parker suggested cabbage soup and chopped liver; both men ordered a second bowl of soup. Kissinger bestowed the ultimate compliment, saying the soup was as good as his mother made.

Alan Dershowitz, the noted law professor and writer, asked Parker's advice on opening a delicatessen in Boston. Parker said, "Alan, you're a brilliant lawyer, but you should stick to what you know." Dershowitz did not heed the counsel and opened up Maven's, which closed in six months, exactly what Parker had predicted.

The Doubting Thomases feared that the Carnegie Deli could not continue serving the same high quality with Leo Steiner gone. But what these skeptics did not realize was that by 1988, the delicatessen ran itself efficiently with an experienced and talented cadre of cooks, countermen, and servers.

The cynics also failed to acknowledge that Parker, after 11 years, had become knowledgeable about the modus operandi of the delicatessen business. He would be the first to admit that he was not a food expert in the training and spirit of his former partner. But he had kept his eyes and ears open and had learned what was needed to maintain high delicatessen quality and service.

Every day in every way, Milton Parker proved he could run the show alone.

THE SMART MOVES

Parker undertook two steps that would enhance the Carnegie Deli's reputation and increase its business. The first was to make the sandwiches two inches taller. The second was to open the Secaucus, New Jersey, commissary with its larger food preparation area. The basement on Seventh Avenue in Manhattan had become too small for the volume of business being done at the deli and by the new branches.

The choice to make the sandwiches higher was based on a business decision. Parker decided to cancel advertising and public relations expenses and transfer those funds into providing extra meat. It was a ledger entry, monies transferred from the expense column into the cost of food column. The bottom line would remain the same.

Parker remembered a valuable lesson learned from his luncheonette business, the story of Topps Chewing Gum. In the 1950s, there were three main bubble gum companies, Topps, Bowman, and Fleer, battling in cutthroat competition for the candy store business.

Topps, however, offered a dozen pencils to the retailer (to sell for a $0.60 profit at a nickel each) or free dishes. The distributor who sold 100 cases received a free electric typewriter.

The extra freebie given by Topps always stayed in Parker's mind. When customers had an option among three or four me-too products, many chose the one that gave away something free. The "free" would be extra meat at the same sandwich price. He also recalled that Mr. Topps lived in a penthouse on Park Avenue, and he could not recall where Mr. Fleer or Mr. Bowman lived.

Parker listened for years to the voices of the people in Carnegie lines, talking about the "big sandwich." He thought that if he could increase the buzz, then word of mouth would

generate more positive publicity than print ads or radio commercials. In effect, the spontaneous chatter about the bigger
sandwiches would become the Carnegie Deli's sole form of
advertising.

Parker had witnessed how the deli's clientele had changed
over the 11 years he and Steiner had operated the deli. The
Max Hudes era could be termed the time of local patrons
living and working in the Carnegie Hall area. After Mimi
Sheraton's review, the deli was transformed into a New York
deli crowd, attracting metropolitan-area diners. By 1988,
American tourists represented the largest percentage of the
deli's clients.

The decision to add two extra inches to the pastrami,
corned beef, and tongue sandwiches represented Parker's smart
way of thinking that when people from Pasadena, or from Jack-
sonville, or from wherever, returned home after a visit to the
Carnegie Deli, they would recount the eating of the humon-
gous sandwich. The diners would retell of their ordering and
fun dining adventure. Yesterday's Carnegie Deli diners would
advertise the restaurant to tomorrow's New York City visitors—at no expense to the Carnegie Deli.

OTHER CARNEGIE DELIS

In the late 1980s and 1990s, the Carnegie Deli embarked on expansion in seven other locations. Only one satellite operation—
at the Food Court at the Sands Casino in Atlantic City—made
money. The conclusions were twofold: the Carnegie Deli's food
product could not be replicated outside of the Seventh Avenue
store, and each new Carnegie Deli needed a Parker or a Steiner
to oversee the restaurant seven days a week.

Parker acknowledged that he was responsible for the failure of the expansions. He said, "I did not know how to run a

multichain operation. I wonder how other restaurants do it?" And he observed, "In the long run, you have to be there all the time. Experienced managers can only do so much; you have to give it attention every day."

Other problems plagued the expansions; the investor partners tried to cut down the Carnegie Deli menu in size. In addition, the satellites purchased less expensive product, from local purveyors and not from the Carnegie's commissary in Secaucus. One Carnegie branch bought just mustard and cheesecake from the commissary.

For Parker, these years were frustrating times. He could not fix what he could not see. He tried to set up the successful New York system, transferring cook Fernando Perez to Chicago and sending New York managers to operate other branches. But no matter how much money was spent (the lion's share put up by the various regional partnerships), eventually the other Carnegie Delis would close one by one.

Out of the flames of expansion failure one component would survive, and it would become the most remunerative part of the operation: the commissary.

The decision to open a retail operation in Secaucus, New Jersey, succeeded in one aspect; the basement area downstairs allowed the curing of the meats to be moved to larger quarters. Parker hired Jeff Jensen to head the commissary operation. Jensen knew how food distributors operated and thought that it might be possible to sell some of the Carnegie's excess cured meat and dessert products wholesale. It was a revolutionary idea, not considered before because of the limited space in New York City.

The start of the wholesale attempt in the mid-1990s was almost invisible. Jensen printed up table-tent cards and set these out on the Carnegie's tables, announcing the wholesale business and instructing would-be buyers to telephone New Jersey.

STILL GOING STRONG

By 1991, there were three remaining business problems to attend to: enlarging the seating capacity on Seventh Avenue, purchasing the building that housed the Carnegie Deli, and buying out the silent partners who owned 20 percent.

Parker was always interested in the stationery store around the corner from the deli. He had indicated to the landlord that he might be interested in assuming the lease if and when the store's lease was up. In 1991, the Carnegie Deli expanded by breaking through the wall and converting the stationery store space into a large back dining room, seating 72 more people.

The arrangement with the silent partners was a standard buyout agreement; either side could make an offer to purchase the other's shares. Over the years, the silent partners had rejected Parker's bids to be bought out. But a number of events had occurred that made the partners think the time was ripe to exit the Carnegie Deli. Leo Steiner was dead, and his 40 percent rested in Parker's hands.

The silent partners presented Parker with their buyout number. Parker's business counsel was always to let the other person present a number first. He studied the deal and took it, although he was suspicious why the partners wanted out, since business was profitable. Doubts aside, he knew that for the next generation to succeed, he needed to own 100 percent of the Carnegie Deli.

A few weeks later, Parker's original suspicions were aroused when he noticed the opening of a delicatessen across the street from the Carnegie Deli on the east side of Seventh Avenue. The new competitor placed a big sign on its awning that said, "Why stay in line [read: the Carnegie's line] when you could be eating now?" The sign had no effect on the Carnegie's business, since people wanted the best delicatessen food and did not mind lining up for a few minutes.

Negotiations to purchase the building that housed the deli (where Parker had the right of first refusal on any sale) continued for many years, and after years of litigation under the savvy guidance of real estate attorney Larry Hutcher, the deal was struck with the heirs of Max Hudes. Parker considered this business transaction as the second most important decision in the deli's history, the hand curing of the meats being the most significant.

The Seventh Avenue location could now accommodate more diners in the back room, which filled on weekends and on many nights for dinners. It had proved to be more than just a larger room for the lunchtime lines.

Summing Up a Career

In 2000, Milton Parker decided to give up the everyday running of the business and concentrate on the larger picture. In the works may be the building of a new and larger commissary and perhaps a branch in Las Vegas.

More than 50 years have passed since Milton Parker's earlier days of penny candy and sandwiches in small luncheonettes. In 1976, circumstance had paired him with Leo Steiner and the then-faded Carnegie Deli in a time of major commercial decline in New York. But events at the deli and in the city also had changed for the better, and both succeeded in spectacular ways no one could have conceived of 30 years ago.

Parker always comes into the deli when he's not in Florida. The staff refers to him as "Mr. Parker," a term of endearing respect. He has imparted to Sandy Levine and to Jeff Jensen the business credo that he has followed his whole life: "Anything that's at fault with the Carnegie Deli is the fault of management and no one else."

The Carnegie Deli serving staff surrounds Milton Parker. Jack Sirota is at the far right.

Over the many years, Parker admitted a fact he learned from thousands of days at the Carnegie Deli. He said, "People eat with their eyes first and then with their mouths."

It's a statement made by a "deli man."

DELI SLANG

Delicatessens and restaurants in New York developed a slang language for ordering. Denizens of Greenwich Village from the 1950s and 1960s will remember the actress/waitress at The Gallery on Christopher Street whose hip, slang performance was as tasty as the sandwiches. She would present the check, asking, "Something more? Something less?" Here are some of the shortcuts used somewhere today:

Pistol	Pastrami
Betty Grable	Cheesecake
Dressed	Russian dressing, coleslaw
Jack	Grilled American cheese, tomato
Wreck 'em	Scrambled eggs
One with	Hot dog with sauerkraut
Brown cow	Chocolate milk
Dry	No butter on the toast
Whiskey	Rye bread
Full house	Grilled cheese with bacon
CB	Corned beef
Grade A	Milk
Draw one	Coffee
Combo	Swiss cheese added to any sandwich
Dutch	American cheese added to any sandwich
Schmear	Cream cheese
Coney	Hot dog
Down	Toast
Seaboard	A takeout order
One off	Plain hot dog

One of the more memorable shortcut meal descriptions came from *The Jackie Gleason Show*. Art Carney was enjoying a bowl of soup when Gleason asked what he was eating. The Carney character replied, "A couple of breadsticks in onion soup." Gleason peered into the bowl and said, "It looks like a logjam in a muddy river to me."

1981: PASTRAMI SANDWICH TO THE RESCUE

This story began in 1655 when Asser Levy, a Jewish citizen of New Amsterdam, volunteered to serve in the newly formed local militia. But local Governor Peter Stuyvesant refused to allow Jewish men to bear arms. Levy appealed to the government in Holland and was permitted to do guard duty. In effect, Levy was the first Jewish policeman in the United States.

Today, one of the most visible Jews in the New York Police Department is Rabbi Alvin Kass, the Chief Chaplain of the NYPD. He has served as the Jewish chaplain for 38 years, after having finished a tour as chaplain in the U.S. Air Force. His congregation for the past 25 years has been the East Midwood Jewish Center in Brooklyn.

In 1981, Rabbi Kass received an emergency call at 11 P.M. that a gun-toting man was holding his girlfriend hostage in a midtown Manhattan office. The police's hostage unit had been unsuccessful in convincing the man to give up the woman and surrender his gun. The man indicated he was Jewish, and spoke about emigrating to Israel.

Rabbi Kass was driven to the office building and seated behind a bulletproof screen to talk to the hostage taker. The Rabbi implored the man to release the woman and to surrender. A dialogue ensued about right and wrong according to Jewish law, but the man did not give up despite the Rabbi's pleading. The talks continued until both men grew hoarse from the lengthy conversation.

At 3:30 A.M., the man revealed that he had not eaten all day and was hungry. The police offered to bring back a hamburger or a pizza, which the man rejected. He wanted a pastrami sandwich on rye.

The police telephoned the Carnegie Deli to order two pastrami sandwiches, one for the hostage taker and one for the rabbi. Rabbi Kass insisted that the man trade his pistol for the pastrami and the man agreed.

When the Carnegie Deli pastrami sandwiches arrived, the man slid his gun under the screen at the same time as he grabbed the sandwich. A moment before the police rushed in for the collar, the man confessed, "Rabbi, I have a second gun."

A few minutes later he said, "This is the best pastrami sandwich I ever ate."

"It's from the Carnegie Deli," said the Rabbi.

Another hour of talks followed. Then the man admitted he was still hungry. Rabbi Kass said, "I have another pastrami sandwich untouched."

"Untouched! Why?" asked the man.

"I keep kosher, and this sandwich is not," replied the rabbi.

The man pondered the statement for a second. "You wouldn't lie to me, would you, Rabbi?"

"No. But the arrangement will be the same as before. One gun for one pastrami sandwich."

"Deal," said the hungry man.

The switch was made as the second gun appeared under the screen. The police waited a beat, then rushed to arrest the man. He complained bitterly that he had not been given enough time to finish his second pastrami sandwich.

Rabbi Kass received a commendation for the fine hostage negotiation work.

It marked the only time a Carnegie Deli sandwich traveled in a police car with the sirens blaring.

1988: BIG TEX MEETS BIG SANDWICH

Texans and tourists agree that a memorable sight at the entrance to the annual Texas State Fair in Dallas is the gigantic figure of a cowboy in a red gingham shirt, blue jeans, and a big western hat known affectionately as Big Tex. On September 9, 1988, Big Tex in the flesh arrived at the Carnegie Deli in the guise of the lean and tall Texas Senator Lloyd Bentsen, the Democratic candidate for vice president of the United States.

Bentsen had just eaten a fund-raiser luncheon at the Tavern on the Green before he showed up at the restaurant. He brought a half-full stomach and Henny Youngman, a supporter who steered clear of any one-liners.

The Carnegie had been telephoned in advance because high-profile people like presidential and vice presidential candidates do not wait in line. Before Bentsen set a foot inside, the deli was "swept" clean by Secret Service agents, the FBI, and some bomb-smelling Alsatian dogs that were under a tight leash not to nosh on the cured meats.

Bentsen ordered a combo sandwich of corned beef and pastrami. When the big sandwich arrived at the table, he pondered the age-old Carnegie Deli question, "How do I eat this?"

For the photo op and for his state's reputation, Bentsen took a big, deep-in-the-heart-of-Texas bite out of the mounds of cured meat. "That's really good," he declared. Then, after the photographers exited, he proceeded to eat the rest of the sandwich with a knife and fork. Local deli patrons were aghast.

In October, when his Republican opponent Dan Quayle said, "I have as much experience in the Congress as Jack Kennedy did when he sought the presidency," Bentsen replied with the now-famous comment: "Senator, I served with Jack Kennedy. I knew Jack Kennedy. Jack Kennedy was a friend of mine. Senator, you're no Jack Kennedy."

Of course, the one remark Bentsen remembered from the losing campaign came from owner Milton Parker, who smiled when Big Tex viewed the big sandwich with awe. He said, "Senator, if you can finish this, you get another one free." Bentsen opted for the one sandwich and a doggy bag.

Parker also gave him a large cheesecake to take back for his staff.

The ever-gracious Bentsen said, "That was some large sandwich combo."

Parker again quipped, "Senator, the combo for two is really dinner for four."

When Bentsen and his wife exited the restaurant carrying doggy bags, the crowd of onlookers behind the barricades cheered him.

"That's the way we do it in New York, Senator," someone shouted, dangling his own Carnegie Deli doggy bag.

1988: Pastrami at Ten Paces

Never underestimate the fervor of native New Yorkers when opinions are divided on local sports teams or competing restaurants. If you want to see blood pressure rise and tempers flare, even today, ask which center fielder was best during the heyday of New York baseball. Was it Mickey Mantle of the New York Yankees, Willie Mays of the New York Giants, or the Brooklyn Dodgers' Duke Snyder?

New York City has never been a one-opinion town; passions have run high ever since Peter Stuyvesant tried to prohibit a small group of Portuguese-speaking Sephardic Jews from entering the seventeenth-century colony of New Amsterdam. The tolerant Dutch patrons of the West India Company overruled him. (The remnant of this first established Jewish community in America can be viewed at St. James Place and Chatham Square at the southern boundary of Chinatown. It is a small graveyard of the Portuguese-American Synagogue, the first of three standing cemeteries in Manhattan.)

The most violent intramural New York City feud occurred in 1849, when blood was shed during a theater spat that began when two competing Shakespearean actors took to the footlights at different theaters on the same night. MacCready, the celebrated Englishman, represented English aristocracy, and Forrest, the American-born, championed the country's working classes. Thousands of irate teenage boys and angry fans of the popular American actor hurled stones and battled New York's 7th Regiment militia until shots were fired into the crowd.

The Seeds of the Pastrami Conflict

People who understood the historical ardor of New Yorkers for their favorite eateries were not surprised when, in July 1988, the first shot was fired in what the media headlines would describe as "The Pastrami Wars." Pitted against each other in cured meat reputation combat for the hearts, minds, and bellies of the New York deli faithful were those two sibling establishments located less than a block apart on Seventh Avenue, the Carnegie Deli and the Stage Deli.

Milton Parker will state with characteristic honesty that the Carnegie Deli lived off the overflow clientele of the more popular Stage Delicatessen. The Stage enjoyed a reputation as the place that first attracted the show business crowd, and also the lines of tourists who wanted to rub elbows with the famous.

The Stage specialized in naming sandwiches after famous people. A diner could enjoy a Jack Benny, a Milton Berle, or a Lucille Ball. The history of the celebrity sandwich began when owner Max Asnas allowed his show business regulars to make their own sandwiches at the deli, piling any combination of meat, fish, vegetables, and condiments atop the bread. He recorded these sometimes bizarre choices and then printed them on the menu with the creator's name.

A New York deli lives or dies with its cured meats reputation. Years after Mimi Sheraton, the *New York Times* restaurant critic, rated the Carnegie one of the three best pastrami delis in the New York metropolitan area, the gloves came off in the confrontation about which pastrami in New York City was the "Tops."

Like the final four teams remaining in the NCAA March basketball tournament, there were four New York deli finalists whose loyal patrons clamored that their deli's pastrami should be crowned city champion. In the finals were Katz's (the oldest deli in New York), the Second Avenue Deli, the Stage, and the reigning winner, the Carnegie.

Everyone in the deli world knew that the bragging rights would be between the Stage and the Carnegie, the uptown rivals located in the center of the tourist and broadcast media districts. The city's publicity spotlight would shine brighter on the glitzy "big name" delis with the show business crowds and out-of-towner notoriety.

The Aftermath of Leo Steiner's Death

The comics started the Stage versus Carnegie heavyweight deli battle a few weeks after Leo Steiner's death. Steiner had welcomed the funnymen with free food and reserved a comedians' table that included special linen (not paper) napkins. He schmoozed with the jokesters; many came in every day to be a part of Leo's Comics' Club. And he picked up tab after tab.

By 1988, people from the heartland and the hinterland made pilgrimages to New York City to see a Broadway show, Radio City Music Hall with the Rockettes, and the Statue of Liberty, and also to have a meal at the Carnegie Deli.

These tourists constituted an ever-increasing percentage of the Carnegie Deli's customer base. They did not care if some second- or third-ranked comic banana sat next to them. They came for the big sandwiches of pastrami and corned beef whose reputation had been enhanced by glowing food reviews and color photographs in their regional magazines and newspapers.

Milton Parker decided that it was time to end the free deli ride for the comedians and replaced their reserved table with a lighted, four-tier, revolving cake stand. It was a not-so-subtle hint that the freebie days of former partner Leo Steiner were over. Parker wanted everyone to realize that business was the main focus of the Carnegie Deli.

One by one, some of the shocked comedians started to drift to the Stage Deli, where they were welcomed with open arms and sour pickles like long-lost family members returning home.

The Mason Jar

Jackie Mason, the well-known comedian, had been a regular diner at the Carnegie Deli for years. Mason was a larger hit in England than he was in America, establishing a record for having given seven command performances in front of the Queen of England.

In July 1988, Mason returned to New York City to mount another show and decided that a terrific way to entertain the glitterati would be to host a midnight deli soiree at the Carnegie. A Mason representative approached Milton Parker with the private party proposal.

Parker rejected the idea outright. He did not want to affront any new or old Carnegie Deli customer with a "Closed Tonight for Private Party" sign. When Mason's representative did not offer to pay for the event, Parker further realized he did not want to return to the Leo Steiner comedians' ritual where they did not pick up a check at the Carnegie Deli.

The rejection steamed Mason. He didn't like being thought of as some cheapskate looking for a free lunch (albeit, in this case, a free midnight supper). What galled him also was that he had mentioned the delights of the Carnegie Deli in numerous past monologues, giving the restaurant wonderful free publicity.

Mason would not suffer the Carnegie's perceived insult; he would take his business to the Stage Deli. And he would announce the defection to the media. Reversing General Douglas

MacArthur's line upon exiting the Philippines, Mason's departure said in effect, "I shall *not* return."

Mason, the comedic big gun, had fired the opening salvo. The Pastrami Wars had erupted into a full-scale tempest in a "glass tea."

Water, Water, Everywhere

The Stage Deli was delighted with the much-publicized imbroglio. Ever since the Carnegie Deli had been judged as having the best pastrami, the Stage had witnessed those long lines forming in front of its uptown rival. And Woody Allen, having chosen the Carnegie for the deli setting of *Broadway Danny Rose*, sent a subtle cinematic message to the country's moviegoers that the place for the best deli food in New York City was the Carnegie.

In a page taken out of a devious medieval tale of backstabbing and intrigue, the Stage Deli hosted Leo Steiner's wife Irma to dine whenever she wanted. She fanned the controversy's flames by stating, "Since Leo died, I don't feel right about going to the Carnegie." Parker did not rise to take the widow's bait and continued to offer her the exclusive linen napkin even if she came into the Carnegie only for cake and coffee.

Then the Stage hurled a calumnious accusation against the Carnegie, known as the "Water shot heard round the world." The Stage said that its pastrami was better than the Carnegie's. The reason why? Because the Stage bought its cured meat from Ben Friedman Meats, which was located in Manhattan and used New York City water in the brine solution, while Carnegie pastrami was cured across the river in the town of Secaucus, committing the scandalous sacrilege of using . . . *water from New Jersey!*

With this truthful revelation, the Stage believed it had dealt the battle-ending blow in the confrontation of the deli heavyweights. It counted on native New Yorkers to boycott the Carnegie in altruistic acts of New York City boosterism. (Much like the locals' 1849 affection for the actor Forrest versus his non-American rival, MacCready.) The Stage had drawn a combative line in the sand and filled it with brine.

The message was clear: "New York City deli lovers, you have driven on the New Jersey Turnpike so you know what that state across the Hudson River offers—horrible and visible chemical tanks polluting the air with pungent smoke." Why would anyone drink New Jersey water, much less use it in brine to cure New York City deli pastrami and corned beef? Why would anyone eat out-of-state Carnegie pastrami when the Stage offered New York City's own?

The Carnegie Deli absorbed the shot the way a great heavyweight takes a solid blow to the solar plexus. Once it had rebounded off the ropes, the Carnegie responded with a flurry of stinging, unanswered jabs.

Parker replied to the Stage by saying, "New Jersey's got great water. Our pastrami is a better product, because we make it ourselves, from *our own recipe.*" Then, with the Stage reeling from the Carnegie's *"our own recipe"* (i.e., Leo Steiner's award-winning method for hand curing with special seasonings) remark, Parker wound up and delivered the knockout blow. He said, "Remember, the Stage Deli *buys* their pastrami."

The choice was obvious: The Carnegie's homemade pastrami was one of a kind and homemade, while the Stage's pastrami could be found at any other New York deli that purchased Ben Friedman Meats.

A Brokered Truce: Meet Me in St. Louis

Could the Pastrami Wars go on as long as the Hundred Years War? The feuding "Sisters on Seventh" were battering New

York's deli capital reputation. Outside negotiators started to appear to reconcile the differences.

The first to offer assistance was lawyer Alan Dershowitz, the Harvard Law School professor who had represented Claus von Bülow in the infamous trial. Both the Stage and the Carnegie rejected Dershowitz's well-intentioned mediation, which appeared as an Op Ed piece in the *New York Times*. The two delis considered that Dershowitz's native Brooklyn deli taste buds might have been diminished by his many years dining on baked scrod in Boston's Durgin Park.

Other, cooler heads decided to bring the warring parties together in a genuine deli lovefest. Then in a peace settlement offer as odd in a sense as Portsmouth, New Hampshire, becoming the site for the treaty of the 1905 Russo-Japanese War, the parties agreed to go to St. Louis. *Nu, St. Louis???*

A businessman named Lester Miller, a St. Louis native, decided to arbitrate the dispute by hosting a "Pastrami War Party" on his large estate west of the City of the Arch. It also provided an excuse to invite Missourians to donate money to the failed presidential run of the state's own representative, Richard Gephardt.

The two delis cooperated by sending pastrami and chopped liver to the deli fest. The deli owners went west also, Louis Auerbach of the Stage and Milton Parker representing the Carnegie. Parker also brought along the faithful Henny Youngman, who had not deserted his beloved delicatessen. Henny provided some one-liners: "I worked in a deli where my boss was so tough he used to stab me good night." And "You want to drive your wife crazy? Don't talk in your sleep—smile."

The 300 guests voted for the best-tasting pastrami by ballots placed in a closed box. Miller never opened the box, and the ballots were not counted. A draw was declared and both deli owners returned to New York with their cured meat and chopped liver reputations intact.

Pastrami Peace Reigns

The Pastrami Wars had ended, and not too soon to suit most New Yorkers. This New York City feud had not witnessed the 7th Regiment militia shouldering rifles aimed at the angry crowds in the street.

Jackie Mason returned as a loyal patron. In 1996, he and his writing partner, the noted divorce attorney Raoul Felder, would praise the Carnegie in their book *Jackie Mason and Raoul Felder's Guide to New York and Los Angeles Restaurants.*

The upshot of the Pastrami Wars was that Milton Parker was now in charge. He would emerge from the shadows of obscurity to become the visible new face and heart of the popular delicatessen.

1989 TO 1994: GOING HOLLYWOOD

Los Angeles is an American city with a large Jewish population. The City of Angels had welcomed a steady stream of Jews from the beginning of the silent film era, when many of the new moviemakers were European immigrants seeking to break into the fledgling industry.

A few New York–style delicatessens greeted these arrivals: Canter's, which had started out in Jersey City, New Jersey, in 1924, moved to Boyle Heights, Los Angeles, in 1931, and then in 1946 to the Fairfax District. The second deli was Nate 'n Al's, opened in Beverly Hills in 1945 by two deli men from Detroit.

Later, Junior's, originally from Brooklyn, would open branches in Encino in the San Fernando Valley and in Westwood, south of the UCLA campus. Much later, the Stage Deli moved into Century City as part of its delicatessen regional expansion.

The question Angelinos asked themselves was this: Did the West Los Angeles/Beverly Hills/Hollywood area need another delicatessen even if it was the famous Carnegie Deli from New York City? Billionaire and deli aficionado Marvin Davis decided that the answer was an unequivocal yes.

The Courtship

Marvin Davis, the oil billionaire, grew up in Manhattan where deli food was a staple of his life. He loved delis and he loved the hardworking men who made serving deli food their life's passion. Most of all, he loved the Carnegie's Leo Steiner.

He regaled the New York owner with the idea that a Carnegie Deli restaurant in posh Beverly Hills would make a bundle—and those sales were just from the meals ordered by the bicoastal members of the Friars Club.

Davis pitched Steiner the idea of a Beverly Hills Carnegie Deli the way a movie studio mogul (which he was since he owned 20th Century Fox) pitched a movie project to a reluctant movie star. He promised that the Hollywood crowd would welcome the famous Carnegie Deli as the new delicatessen messiah. Beverly Hills could be the Promised Land for the next Carnegie Deli satellite restaurant. And to sweeten the deal, Davis would put his money—lots of it—where his mouth was.

How often had Steiner heard returning comedians and show business people complain, "Leo, there's no good deli in Los Angeles." Steiner could not resist the tempting offer. For the record, Milton Parker was less enthusiastic about the potential of a Southern California-based Carnegie Deli.

The Setup

Marvin Davis had the clout and the cash to find a prime restaurant location on North Beverly Hills Drive. He hired the well-known restaurant interior designer Pat Kuleto to design the two spacious rooms, which one wag said looked more like a movie set of what a deli should look like than a real New York deli. It was Art Deco and attractive in its way, but it did not resemble New York delis that had accumulated real atmosphere and cured-meat aromas for years.

Davis enlisted the participation of the old comics in the deli venture, appointing the venerable and beloved George Burns chairman of the board. Milton Berle reported that he owned 2 percent. Davis's smart idea was to re-create Steiner's comedians' table, to make the West Coast Carnegie Deli the new show business clubhouse where former Borscht Belt and radio comics would rub elbows with the tourists eager to do some star spotting and some serious deli dining.

To publicize the announcement, Davis persuaded Milton Parker to send gift packages of Carnegie deli food to megastars like Streisand and other big names in Hollywood.

The New York Carnegie Deli sent out an experienced manager in the person of Bob Trager, who had been the deli's general manager back on Seventh Avenue for seven years. He was a manager to the deli world born, the grandson of the owner of the famous New York appetizer store landmark, Murray's Sturgeon Shop.

Leo Steiner died before ever seeing the opening of the West Coast Carnegie Deli branch.

The Opening

On August 9, 1989, the Carnegie Deli Beverly Hills opened its doors at 7 A.M. to a huge line waiting to enter. By 7 P.M., more than 2,000 people had stopped by in what the *Los Angeles Times* would describe as "the most hyped deli opening in history."

The newspaper's statement proved no exaggeration; the long expectation for this famous deli's first-day performance rivaled any Hollywood star-filled nighttime premiere reserved for the opening of a multimillion-dollar motion picture. Everyone in town anticipated the Carnegie Deli would be a blockbuster and do boffo business.

On that first day also, *Variety's* Army Archerd stood out front greeting familiar faces as though he were welcoming movie stars arriving on Oscar night. All the local television stations sent crews to cover the all-day event. The media were everywhere, interviewing celebrities, chatting to the repatriated Brooklynites and Bronxites, and questioning the local folk who had no link back to the New York deli experience.

Inside it was the dynamic and electric mix of delicatessen and show business: Carol Channing, the well-known Broadway musical star, dropped a huge matzoh ball the size of a basketball into an enormous bowl of chicken soup. Barbara and Marvin Davis sliced a six-foot salami in lieu of a tape-cutting ceremony.

The Curtain Comes Down

On November 16, 1994, the Beverly Hills Carnegie Deli was dark. A reporter for the *New York Times* wrote, "After several lean years, it became increasingly clear that this Carnegie could not cut the mustard."

Five years after the opening, the branch had suffered less-than-spectacular reviews about the food and the personnel (some greenhorn waiters and waitresses could not recognize the difference between pastrami and corned beef). *LA Zagat's Guide*—the restaurant voice of the people—claimed the deli served "flat food."

In the five years in business, the deli never met the investors' high expectations. Over time, Marvin Davis and Milton Parker did not see eye to eye on how to maintain standards established for years in the New York store. Parker also had to listen to the returning crowd that grumbled about the West Coast establishment, "Milton, there's *still* no good deli in Los Angeles."

The blame game began and then the finger pointing. But this exercise proved futile and unrewarding. Davis had enjoyed the ultimate deli experience, the dream of owing a delicatessen, of naming sandwiches after friends and cronies, and of walking around the kitchen sampling the food. He had poured big money into the restaurant, but even someone worth billions of dollars realized it was time to close the show for good.

The critics, with 20-20 hindsight, said it was impossible to recreate the 50-plus-year-old New York Carnegie Deli in modern, palm-tree-lined Beverly Hills. By the time this West Coast satellite closed in 1994, Parker had also closed Chicago, Secaucus, Atlantic City, Fort Lauderdale, and the short-lived Scottsdale.

On the day the door closed forever in Beverly Hills, there was a line of patrons waiting to eat outside Nate 'n Al's Delicatessen. It had thrived as the deli of choice for the Los Angeles show business folk and the New York expatriate crowd. The Mendelsohn family had made it as beloved to its customers as the Carnegie Deli was to native New Yorkers. There was a good business lesson in that.

1991: SIMON SAYS

Imagine if you were held hostage for 40 days and nights by an antagonistic Iraqi military that considered you a spy. What American food would you crave when and if you were released?

For CBS's *60 Minutes* ace reporter Bob Simon, that answer was easy: one Carnegie Deli pastrami and corned beef combination sandwich.

Turn back the pages of time to January 1991 and the Gulf War. Simon and a three-person crew were covering the conflict when they were captured by an Iraqi patrol inside the border of Kuwait.

Although the crew insisted it was on a journalistic assignment—with documentation, identification, and cameras to prove it—the Iraqis believed the four men were spies. The men, reporter Simon; Peter Bluff, a producer; Roberto Alvarez, cameraman; and soundman Juan Caldera, were taken at gunpoint to Baghdad and placed inside a military intelligence prison, the now infamous Abu Ghraib hellhole.

In captivity, the crew was threatened with death, blindfolded, and often beaten with canes and sticks. Twenty-four of the 40 days were spent in solitary confinement. The prison was subject to three allied bombing missions, and the Americans feared death from their own military's air raids.

Then, one day, other Iraqi officials drove the men to the Al Rashid hotel in Baghdad. Later, they were driven to the Jordanian border and then flown to England.

In London, Simon revealed a craving to CBS President Eric Goldberger for a Carnegie Deli combo known as the Woody Allen. He said that while he was in solitary confinement—and being ill fed—his mind kept returning to the delicious Carnegie Deli pastrami and corned beef combo. Years before the Gulf War, whenever Simon stayed overnight in the New York City hotel district of the West Fifties, he had eaten often at the Carnegie Deli and referred to it with much affection as "my private cafeteria."

Goldberger telephoned the Carnegie, which prepared four corned beef and pastrami combos, added cheesecake and fudge cake, and included Cel-Ray sodas. The shipment was airlifted by the Concorde and arrived in England the next day.

The sandwiches were rushed to the London hospital where the former hostages were kept for observation. The one medical finding was that the men were malnourished.

A memorable photograph of bearded Bob Simon eating the sandwich shows the intense and comforting pleasure of a man who had undergone a terrible ordeal and survived to tell the tale.

When Simon returned to New York City, one of his first stops was to thank the Carnegie Deli's owners for their kindness. As he walked into the restaurant, the staff recognized their regular customer and burst into impromptu applause. There was not a dry eye in the place.

1999: OMAHA STEAKS

In 1997, Steve Simon, the VP and general manager of the well-known Omaha Steaks' catalog and retail outlets, returned again to his favorite delicatessen in New York City, the Carnegie Deli. He spied a table-tent card and noticed that it mentioned the sale of products for wholesale businesses.

Omaha Steaks, in business since 1917 and in its fifth-generation as a family-owned company, searched for exciting and profitable new food items to add to its catalog and retail stores. The Carnegie Deli cheesecake seemed to meet those requirements.

Simon introduced himself to Sandy Levine, whose knowledge of Omaha Steaks was minimal. A New Yorker has access to some of the world's best butchers and local steak houses, and little need of purchasing top quality meats by mail order from as far away as Nebraska.

Levine pointed out that the Carnegie was selling some of its cheesecakes in a Saks Fifth Avenue catalog.

"How many in the Saks mailing?" asked Simon.

"Lots and lots," replied Sandy. "Around 45,000."

Simon had to restrain from giggling out loud. Omaha Steaks mailed 1.6 million pieces at least twice a year to an existing list of "good" customers and many more millions to prospective customers annually. He also knew by memory the percentage of items ordered per each mailing based on years of mail order history. He recognized that 45,000 pieces would generate few sales of an item as unique as cheesecake, especially in a catalog for a department store known for its fine line of clothing.

Levine showed Simon how the pastrami and corned beef were steamed downstairs and then sliced, assuming a meat company like Omaha Steaks might be interested in selling the cured meats.

When Simon asked where the meats and the cheesecakes were prepared, Levine took him to the commissary on Avenue D on the Lower East Side, a part of town that Simon had never visited in New York City before (and has not returned to since).

The warehouse building in Alphabet City was in a part of New York with many dilapidated and uninhabited buildings. To Simon, the exterior did not broadcast pristine quality, a necessary food requirement to be considered in the elegant and respected Omaha Steaks catalog.

Simon followed Levine inside and discovered the bad news. Although the 6,000-square-foot production area was spotless and USDA approved, it was not large enough to supply the number of cheesecakes that Omaha Steaks could sell. The good news was meeting Jeff Jensen, whose baking and management background exuded food professionalism. Simon handed Jensen his business card and said, "Jeff, if you ever expand into larger, make that much larger, facilities, give me a call."

In 1999, when the Carnegie Deli's commissary in Carlstadt, New Jersey, finished an operational and production test period, Jensen telephoned Simon, inviting him to inspect the new facility. Simon came East with Jackie Thompson, the product development manager, and both liked what they saw. The facility was immaculate and the handmade cheesecakes rolled off an efficient assembly line. The Carnegie commissary could promise Omaha Steaks volume and quality.

Although Jensen had never supplied product to a mail order catalog, he understood the special needs of shipping in bulk and offering a fair price for volume business. Both he and Thompson agreed that to maximize sales, the Carnegie Deli name had to appear in the catalog. It marked the first time that Omaha Steaks cobranded an item with a recognizable food maker.

The first Carnegie Deli cheesecakes appeared in 8-inch and 12-inch sizes in the "Holiday Gift Bag" edition of the 1999 Omaha Steaks general catalog. The 700 Omaha Steaks operators waited for orders. The first appearance of a Carnegie Deli cheesecake proved a winner.

Omaha Steaks has always tested different premium offers to increase sales, including other meats and food items. In 2000, the company decided to use a 4-inch Carnegie Deli cheesecake as a free promotional gift when a consumer purchased a specific minimum dollar amount from the catalog. To take full advantage of the Carnegie name, the envelope for the mail piece advertised and displayed in color the Carnegie Deli cheesecake.

The cheesecake promotion proved a big hit, and Omaha Steaks has continued to repeat the offer at least once a year. Jackie Thompson said, "We have a quality story to tell and we like to include quality food items with their own story to tell. That's why the Carnegie Deli cheesecake fits our operation perfectly."

In 2002, Jeff Jensen, pleased with the new wholesale arrangement, flew to Omaha, carrying with him a complete Carnegie Deli lunch, including matzoh ball soup, pastrami, corned beef, rye bread, Russian dressing, pickles, and, of course, cheesecake. Ten Omaha Steaks staffers delighted in the authentic taste of famous New York deli.

Today, the Carnegie Deli cheesecakes are also sold in the 63 Omaha Steaks retail stores throughout the country. Customers interested in sending a cheesecake to friends can order from these locations.

Jeff Jensen hopes that one day Omaha Steaks might sell some of the Carnegie Deli cured meats through its catalogs and retail stores. He said, "What I did not realize from the beginning was the residual benefit to the Carnegie Deli restaurant from the catalog mailings. Omaha Steaks succeeded in making us top of mind when their customers come to New York. It's been terrific advertising for us."

WANT AN OMAHA STEAKS CATALOG?

Go online at www.OmahaSteaks.com or telephone (800) 228-9055. You can locate the nearest retail shop here, also.

2000: HOLD THAT LINE

It was a warm Saturday morning in June, and Marian and Sandy Levine were relaxing at their Long Island home when the telephone rang. The call came from Chuck Smith, Sandy's son-in-law and the weekend manager of the Carnegie Deli. His next statement sent shudders down Sandy's spine: "President Clinton is coming for dinner this evening."

If you are a restaurant owner out on the tip of Long Island and the president of the United States favors your delicatessen with an impromptu visit, it's prudent to return to Manhattan.

They hired a helicopter service and did not wait to take the Hampton Jitney back to Manhattan.

While they were en route, the Carnegie Deli was "swept" by the FBI and the Secret Service. This represented the fourth time that the restaurant had been checked from top to bottom: for Henry Kissinger, Senator Lloyd Bentsen, Vice President Al Gore, and now for President Clinton.

The reservation was made for 7:30 P.M., when some other presidential staffers and Mia Farrow would join the president.

At around 6:30 P.M., the usual dinnertime line began to form in front of the Carnegie Deli. To any New Yorker or, for that matter, to out-of-towners who had eaten at the Carnegie Deli, the line meant one thing: People were waiting for their turn to eat at the restaurant.

However, for the men in black in the Secret Service, the line meant something else: People had assembled to catch a glimpse of the president as patriotic crowds had done for decades. For obvious security reasons, the line of greeters could not remain outside the deli. The people were too close to the restaurant's one door. The line would have to move.

The Secret Service instructed the people waiting in line to move across the street, to walk to the other side of Seventh Avenue. The men explained that President Clinton would be arriving in a short while to eat dinner at the Carnegie.

The people waiting were tourists from out of town who responded to the request at first with surprise and then with resentment. There was the collective perception that if they moved across the street, they would lose their places in the Carnegie Deli line.

"Are you going to save our places in line after the president is seated?" asked one hopeful person.

"No, we can't do that," answered a Secret Service agent. "It's not part of our job."

The crowd started to murmur cries of protest. One by one, the people identified themselves, and offered other biographical information.

"We're the Fielding family from Berkeley, California, and we've planned on eating here for two years."

"I'm Mrs. Pansaci from Buffalo. I promised my two daughters a visit to the Carnegie."

"We're Zabalo and Amat, businessmen from Spain. We read about this restaurant on the Internet. We shall lose our place."

"You have to move," shouted the Secret Service. "The president of the United States is coming. You can see him from across the street."

"We're not here to see the president. We're lined up to eat at the Carnegie Deli."

The Secret Service was surprised to hear this.

"We're not moving," one brave person shouted back. One by one, everyone on the line picked up the cry. No one budged.

"We're the Lippman-Kellys and we're holding theater tickets. Our plans are to eat a quick sandwich and make an 8 P.M. curtain," voiced one irate couple.

"We're the Hummels who've come from Kentucky."

"I'm Dr. Chase, a lifelong Democrat. I voted for Bill Clinton twice, but he has no right to make me miss a dinner at the Carnegie," said a bearded gentleman.

A Secret Service person relayed the unexpected pickle of a predicament back to the president's staff. A sensible person realized that if the Secret Service forced the line to move across the street, it would be the hot, lead story on the nightly television news. Newspaper headlines of "Clinton Cuts in Front of Carnegie Deli Line" would be bad publicity in the next day's New York City tabloids.

President Clinton canceled his reservation and ate at another restaurant in Manhattan.

The line held. Not even the president of the United States could induce these deli lovers from their appointed Carnegie Deli dining rounds.

In 2001, a year after his second term ended, Bill Clinton and daughter Chelsea returned to the Carnegie Deli for the missed meal. He said, "It's delicious. I waited a long time for this dinner."

2001: Murder above the Deli

On the balmy evening of May 10, Sandy Levine left Gracie Mansion, the mayor of New York City's official residency, after a fund-raising dinner. He hailed a cab and headed back to his apartment when he heard the horrifying words on the taxi's radio, "a mass murder committed above the Carnegie Deli."

His heart was in his mouth and his blood pressure shot through the roof. Had the announcer said "*in* the Carnegie Deli"? Or, had he said what he thought he heard, "*above* the Carnegie Deli"? The "in" would mean a horrible calamity had occurred on the premises. The "above" signaled an incident in one of the six rented apartments in the building owned by another Carnegie Deli corporation.

When he arrived at Seventh Avenue and West 55th Street, the entire block had become a police crime scene. Familiar yellow tape roped off the entire street. Police personnel and vehicles were everywhere on the streets and ambulances, also.

The Carnegie Deli was closed. No employee was present. At least this confirmed that the murders had not occurred inside the landmark restaurant.

A large crowd of the curious gathered on the perimeter of the crime scene. Sandy pushed his way through the throng of onlookers until he reached a uniformed policeman. He identified himself as the manager of the Carnegie Deli and asked to speak to a homicide detective.

"Why?" asked the cop. "This is a murder investigation, and no one is allowed in the deli."

"I don't want to go into the deli," Sandy said. "I want to show the police the surveillance videos of the hallway, which are in my office on the third floor."

"Wait here."

A few minutes later, a detective listened to Sandy's surprising revelation. The video system that taped various locations in the deli also kept one camera on the lower landing stairwell. The detective called headquarters, asking for permission to bring an outside person into the building. Permission was granted.

Sandy and Chief Detective Alle entered the Carnegie Deli's office. Sandy found the tape of the hallway and rewound it. The button was pressed to run, and in a short while two men were seen mounting the steps to go upstairs. The videotape was fast-forwarded and the same two men were seen running down the steps. The Carnegie Deli's video camera had caught the murderers on tape.

On May 19, *America's Most Wanted* television show broadcast the faces of the two men. On May 20, one of the suspects turned himself in to the police. A rebroadcast on July 14 assisted in the capture of the second suspect, arrested in Miami. Both men were tried and convicted of murder and robbery.

Chief Detective Alle complimented the Carnegie Deli. The videotape had proved to be a serendipitous piece of good fortune. In its 13th season, *Law and Order* filmed a similar episode using the outside of the restaurant as a backdrop.

Said a weary Sandy Levine, "It was publicity we could have gladly done without."

2003: LIGHT IN THE DARKNESS

Around 4 P.M. on the afternoon of August 15, Sandy Levine was ending his shift at the Carnegie Deli to return to his apartment for a short nap before heading to a benefit performance at Madison Square Garden.

At 4:15 P.M., the lights in the deli went out. At first, Sandy thought a fuse had blown in the building. But a deliveryman entered yelling, "The power is gone in the city!" Sandy exited the deli out into Seventh Avenue and saw that the lights of stores and restaurants were out, including the traffic lights.

Portable battery-powered radios broadcast the upsetting news that a massive power outage had rippled across a wide swath of the Eastern and Midwestern states and also Canada. No one knew when the power would be restored.

Sandy's first decision, and the most important one, was to try to keep the deli open as late and as long as possible. Outside, he sensed a growing panic among people wandering in the street. These were outer borough and suburban commuters who would not be able to return home by train, subway, and PATH service. And he noticed stranded tourists unable to go back to their nearby hotel rooms because elevators did not run.

Sandy assessed the state of affairs for the delicatessen. It had a small backup generator that would last for a few hours. The generator would keep exit signs lit, and it would also illuminate the Carnegie Deli sign out front.

Food in the refrigerators would start to go bad. The steam tables—operated by gas—could continue to cook meat. The Carnegie Deli could remain open into the night if it could find enough candles for the tables.

Sandy outlined a three-part sequential plan—a triage emergency system—based on food supply and potential for spoilage. First, the Carnegie Deli would serve the already made salads and cold fish. The second phase would kick in after the cold plates had been eaten when the cured meats would be steamed and then served as sandwiches (there was an ample supply of bread). For the final step, eggs and milk were placed into the large ice making machines, filled already with ice, with the expectation that, even as the ice melted, the dairy products would retain enough cold and not go bad.

One by one, other restaurants in the vicinity started to close. Without steam tables, there was no point in staying open. Soon the Carnegie and the pizza parlors (also equipped with gas ovens) were the only food-serving places open in the city.

Sandy instructed the deliverymen to buy as many candles as they could find from nearby stores to back up the delicatessen's candle supply. He ordered the countermen to begin cutting the cured meat by hand since the slicing machines did not work. Loaves of bread were also hand sliced into sandwich size.

In walked police chaplain Rabbi Kass (of the 1981 hostage taking) who narrated a touching story. He and his wife, Miriam, had come into Manhattan to celebrate their 40th wedding anniversary. The couple had agreed to meet at the Midtown North Precinct, where, currently, his wife rested on a couch. Sandy offered him a tuna sandwich, an egg cream, and cheesecake, which were also prepared for the hungry Miriam. The Rabbi gave a blessing of thanks to the Carnegie Deli and then rushed to present his wife with her ruby wedding anniversary dinner.

Over time, when people understood that there would be few places to buy food, they headed to the open Carnegie Deli. Each new entrant asked, "Are you open?" or "Are you serving food?" The answer was, "Yes, but just salads. No sandwiches, no eggs, and no cooked dinners."

Inside, Sandy set up a simplified system for ordering food. The patrons were handed a check that they paid at the cash register. Since the cash register could not function without electricity, the Carnegie used an old cigar box. After the diners paid, they returned to the counter and showed the paid checks to the server.

A local radio station, 1010 WINS, telephoned the deli to inquire about ordering food. It could remain broadcasting all night with an emergency generator. Sandy bartered with the station manager: a large platter of food for the station if its announcers mentioned the Carnegie Deli was open with a limited food menu.

By 9 P.M., the Carnegie's candles were running low. Sandy telephoned the police community officer at the Midtown North precinct with an urgent request for more candles. He emphasized that the Carnegie remained the one restaurant open on Seventh Avenue. He had a steady stream of customers with more hungry people waiting outside.

At 10 P.M., the deli ran out of salads and fish and began to serve pastrami, corned beef, and tongue. Patrons did not mind that the sodas were not cold; food, any food with a warm beverage was a better option than going hungry. Some ordered takeout sandwiches and went to eat in Central Park, which seemed cooler than staying inside in the unair-conditioned deli.

The police arrived with new boxes of candles. The sandwich serving continued until 2 A.M. when the Carnegie Deli had run out of meat, sodas, and whatever else it had left over. By that time also, people stranded in the city found someplace to sleep on benches in Central Park or on the floors of Grand Central and Penn Stations.

The Carnegie staff found various places inside the deli to sleep. Sandy could not return to his apartment and decided to sleep outside on this hot and humid night. He set a large cardboard box on the sidewalk and dozed off. At daybreak, he awoke in time to see a man approaching him. The man, thinking Sandy was a homeless person, kicked his legs to get his attention, then said, "Hey, pal, this is for you," and flipped Sandy a quarter. Another Good Samaritan in the city.

At 4:15 A.M., the lights started to go on at the deli, which was in the electric power grid perimeter between West 50th Street and West 57th Street and Sixth and Seventh Avenues. This was the rectangle in the heart of the city's hotel business, and the decision was made to power up the hotels first with their inoperable elevators, which had left thousands of tourists cut off from their rooms.

Sandy woke everyone up. The staff cleaned themselves up as best as they could. At 6:30 A.M., a scant 30 minutes later than the normal opening time, the Carnegie opened its doors for a limited breakfast menu of eggs, toast, and coffee. The eggs and milk had remained colder than anticipated in the big ice machines. The electricity powered the coffeemaker and the toaster.

WINS had made the announcement during the night that the Carnegie would be open for breakfast. At 6:30, a line had already formed outside. Many of the people had slept in the parks or on the streets and were happy for anything to eat. The commissary in New Jersey called, asking if it should make the regular delivery; it had not suffered any loss in power across the river. Sandy said yes. He wanted to be prepared for a busy day.

The power was restored in the city, area by area. The Carnegie's afternoon staff started to show up; some came by car and others by taxi. Sandy sent the night workers home in cabs and limos. The delivery arrived from the commissary on time.

Later in the morning, Sandy walked back to his apartment, where the electricity had also been restored. He showered and shaved, took a quick nap, and returned to work.

The Carnegie Deli had stayed open, feeding as many people as possible, while most restaurants in the city closed. For many, the familiar Carnegie Deli's blinking neon sign was the one beacon of welcoming light on a dark street in a dark, down, but not out for the count, New York City.

The Carnegie Deli had charged its normal prices. Thanks to Sandy's savvy triage of available food, it did not have to turn away any customer and continued serving until the last slices of cured meat were sold. His reward would be the satisfaction of helping out New Yorkers and tourists who would one day be asked the question, "Where were you in the Blackout of 2003?" Many would answer with gratitude, "I ate at the Carnegie Deli."

And Sandy's reward would also include a 25-cent tip.

1988 TO 2004: PROMOTIONS AND AWARDS

With Leo Steiner gone, Milton Parker knew he had to generate some good public relations and hired the PR firm of Howard Rubenstein. The account person assigned to the Carnegie Deli was the talented Dan Klores. He had already worked with the Carnegie for a number of years, until Parker increased the size of the sandwiches and discontinued publicity and advertising.

When New York Mets catcher Gary Carter was in a home run slump in 1988 and needed a pepper-upper to hit his 300th homerun, the Carnegie Deli suggested *Mets-a-Ball* soup. Milton Parker said, "The Deli's *Mets-a-Ball* soup will melt in Carter's mouth, make his bones feel young again, and give him back the soothing power and confidence he needs."

Two other promotions occurred in that year, the "I Want to Be David Letterman's Girlfriend Contest" and Henny Youngman presiding over the "King of the Knish" tasting event.

In 1988, the Carnegie Deli also ran the "Best Jewish Mother" contest (one might think at its own peril). The winner was Mrs. Betty Dickerman of Brooklyn. Arnie Dickerman was the good son who wrote in his mother's name. He said his mother deserved the prize because she took a 1954 slipcover and turned it into a seat cover for the family's 1966 Chevy.

When the car cloth started to fray, she cut it into strings to tie on the bags of recycled garbage. The prize was a $100 check, flowers, and a large salami.

In a 1990 issue of *Premiere* magazine, the Carnegie Deli was the restaurant in the rear of a photograph of a Teenage Mutant Ninja Turtle. (Could the turtle have been Donatello, and had he just come out into the street having eaten a big Carnegie Deli salad?)

In the 1992 Democratic Party convention, held in New York, the Carnegie Deli invented these sandwich combinations: *The Bill Clinton:* corned beef and mayo on white bread; *The Jerry Brown:* ham and baloney combo. For the two other candidates, there was *The George H. W. Bush:* tuna, chopped egg, and mayo on white. (Milton Parker stated that the 41st president's sandwich contained no meat, "Just like the economy.") And *The Ross Perot:* turkey with coleslaw and Russian dressing. (Parker joked again, "It's the sandwich for a gobbler who says nothing.")

In 1995, New York State First Lady Libby Pataki, wife of the governor, named the Carnegie Deli a New York City landmark, honoring it with the state's WHY I LOVE NY Award.

In 1996, Bozo the Clown celebrated his 50th birthday at the Carnegie Deli with a not-so-unusual request: He wanted his own sandwich called the "Bozo Wowie Kazowie." This concoction would include rye bread, jack cheese, pastrami, corned beef, turkey, lettuce, tomato, coleslaw, and Russian dressing topped off by a cherry tomato to represent the famous clown's bright red nose.

In 1999, Ivana Trump (whom the staff consider a most gracious and pleasant lady) stopped in to promote Kraft Deli Deluxe cheese. She ate a combo sandwich made up of cured meats and Kraft cheese. But more interesting than the promotion was the photograph of the smiling Ivana and sandwich-eating Sandy Levine in the May 26 *New York Post*.

In 2002, the deli created a sandwich for beefy Mets first baseman Mo Vaughn, consisting of corned beef, pastrami, turkey, and Swiss cheese. The concoction was called the "Mo-licious."

In 2004, what was good for Kraft was good for Finlandia cheese, which staged the final judging of its National Sandwich Recipe Contest at the Carnegie Deli. The winning entry was called "The Dakota" and was submitted by Bob Durant of New Jersey. The ingredients: chicken salad, raisins, almonds, dried cranberries, crisp bacon slices, and Finlandia Swiss Cheese on a submarine sandwich roll.

Sandy Levine was a judge on the panel along with food editors of various newspapers and journals.

THE BAGEL

In the United States, the bagel has become an all-purpose, tasty, and healthy product that merits its own separate food history section. The recounting will include its history, a biography of Bob Orzo the Bagel Man and his New York City bagel shop, and expert instructions for the best way to make that brunch delicacy: the toasted bagel, lox, and cream cheese combination.

An interesting statistic is that in California, the bagel in all its fresh and frozen formats is the supermarket industry's second-most-purchased food item, ranking next below orange juice. Years ago, the bagel surpassed doughnuts in popularity and volume as the number one U.S. supermarket baking specialty item.

History

The origins of that first-made bagel are lost in Eastern European baking history. However, there are two theories, both with Polish associations. The first comes from a 1610 regulation from the town of Krakow that required pregnant women to be given bagels, probably because of their children who would then teethe on bagels.

The second and more romantic word derivation—the one with the explanation for the why is there a hole question— traces the first bagel to an unknown Viennese baker. He wanted to honor Poland's King Jan, who had succeeded in halting the Turkish invasion of Eastern Europe. Because King Jan smote the infidels on horseback, the baker shaped the yeast into a stirrup-like shape of a not-so-perfect circle.

The German word for stirrup is *Steigbügel* but the old Austrian term was just *Bügel*. Fortunately, *Bügel* became bagel in English and not steigbagel.

Cheesy Developments in the United States

The bagel recipe came to America on the same boat as every other Eastern European Jewish food, and then settled in New York and Chicago. New bakeries made bagels and bialys (a bagel variation) for the millions of newly arrived immigrants.

Bagel makers would shout hosannas of praise for that day in 1872 when a dairyman in Chester, New York, made a "richer cheese than ever before" from cream and whole milk. The popularity of this light and tasty cheese (no pungent cheese odor, either) reached A. L. Reynolds, who in 1880 began to market little bricks of cream cheese in tinfoil wrapping, calling it Philadelphia Cream Cheese.

Why did Reynolds—who wasn't from the City of Brotherly Love—name it Philadelphia since the cheese was not made in that city? The answer is that during the latter part of the nineteenth century, Philadelphia had developed a reputation for making quality food products, which were frequently referred to as being of "Philadelphia quality." Today, of course, the city is better known for housing the Liberty Bell and for William Claude (W. C.) Fields' epitaph, "On the whole, I'd rather be in Philadelphia."

The Union

In 1910, as more people discovered the delights of spreading cream cheese (a *schmear* in Yiddish) on a bagel, the high demand for their production resulted in the formation of the nation's first Bagel Bakers Union, Local #388. A surprising fact about this union comprised of 300 men was that only their sons could ever become union members, to ensure that the secret of rolling and making bagels remained within a small circle of people.

Years ago, baking teams, working in twos and fours, prepared the dough and shaped the bagels into the familiar round shape, then boiled and baked them. The bakers were paid for piecework, and a team could make more than 6,000 bagels in a night's shift.

The tradition of individually hand rolling bagels proved adequate when consumption was primarily confined to the narrow eastern corridor of the United States, with its sizable Jewish population. But two events occurred that would change bagel making in the United States forever. In 1955, Lender's Bakery in New Haven, Connecticut (formed in 1926 by Harry Lender from Poland), started to sell bags of wrapped bagels directly from the supermarket (just like loaves of wrapped bread), and, in 1960, Dan Thompson invented the automatic bagel-making machine.

The newly found demand for bagels by non-Jewish families throughout the United States heralded that bagels were for everyone. Consumers could now purchase bagels in supermarkets wrapped, frozen, or freshly made in baking departments. Or they could go to the newly started bagel shops (or chains of bagel shops) that began to sprout all over the country.

In 1972 in New York City, brothers-in-law Helmer Toro and Hector Hernandez opened H&H Bagels, which soon became the high standard for the New York bagel. The Carnegie Deli buys its bagels from this large and successful operation.

After the Thompson machine became the industry standard (it and other automated machines could produce 400 bagels an hour), the aging bagel makers of Local #388 faded into obscurity. But the old-timers had one last task remaining, to pass on their unique skills. And whom did they instruct in the art of this artisan pastime? The answer is a surprise: men eager and willing to learn in Thailand!

Sometime in the 1990s the government of Thailand requested that members of the dwindling Local #388 come to Thailand to teach bagel-making skills to local residents. For reasons that are not clear, the government perceived that the country should encourage a nascent bagel-making industry for local consumption. The last members of the Bagel Bakers Union were delighted that someone wanted to learn the old skills.

Over time, the demand for handmade bagels never reached the high levels envisioned by the Thai government. The trained sons of the skilled Thai bagel makers could not find work in their native country. What did these professional bagel rollers do? They immigrated to the United States with these unique skills.

The Bagel Man Baketh

At 5 A.M. in the morning, Bob Orzo, the owner of Hudson Bagels on Hudson Street at Christopher Street in Greenwich Village, lights the bagel oven, which needs 45 minutes to heat. When the big pot of water begins to boil in 30 minutes, he will start the bagel-making day at 5:45 A.M.

First, he takes out the bagels rolled the night before and plops these into a 60-gallon kettle of boiling water. The term is called "kettling" the bagels. In a few minutes, the bagels float like ravioli. They are dried for a few minutes. The next step is to add on the seeds, salt, or other toppings. The key is to ensure that one side has a lot of coating, while the flip side has less. (*Note:* The bialy, the poorer cousin to the bagel, is made with softer dough, onions, and no hole, and importantly, is not boiled. For more information on the old European ways of making bread, read Mimi Sheraton's book *The Bialy Eaters.*)

Orzo places five bagels of the same variety on a specially made two-inch by four-inch bagel board that is covered with a strip of canvas cloth. He will set the bagel boards individually on each of the seven rotating baking shelves. A push of the button and the shelves begin to circle slowly like a Ferris wheel inside the Middleby Marshall conveyer oven at a temperature of 525 degrees. The first ride will last four minutes, and then the bagel boards are flipped and the second side rotates for eight minutes. Then, the hot bagels are shaken off their canvas cloth into their individual bins in the front of the store.

Orzo started in the food service business when he was 12 years old, helping his parents in their Queens delicatessen. Coincidentally, he leased the little shop on Hudson from the same restaurant brokers who partnered Leo Steiner with Milton Parker in 1976.

Orzo had never made nor sold fresh bagels, but he saw the store as an opportunity to learn the business, and to try out his passion for organic soups. He decided to make the best bagels by asking old friends from his Queens youth who owned the successful Utopia Bagels. They gave him tips and advice for two weeks. He then hired a professional bagel maker to teach him the art of rolling bagels.

The bagels are made with the authentic, best-quality original recipe: high-gluten flour for the best texture and mixed with barley malt (the reason why a good bagel has a light coffee color), water, yeast, salt, and a touch of brown sugar. Orzo keeps the bagels at the right (or smaller) size. He hopes that the country's fad for things big that created the attack of the mega muffins never happens to the bagel.

Customers' bagel preferences follow: plain, sesame, and the everything bagel. These three varieties represent more than 50 percent of volume. Then comes poppy (oddly, more sold when made with lox), onion, garlic, salt (dropping in popularity), raisin, pumpernickel, rye (made with rye flour), marble rye, and whole wheat. Although Orzo can roll his own bagels, he uses the expert services of a Thai roller who can do in 15 hours what would take the owner 40 hours to accomplish. The bagel rollers are the last of the wandering journeymen who go from bagel store to bagel store in the five boroughs of New York City. They are paid by how many bagels they roll.

Orzo's goal is still to bring his special recipe organic soups to New Yorkers. Currently, he is looking for a larger store uptown on the West Side. But he has no intention of abandoning his bagel business. He intends to offer the soups with the bagels, a perfect combination.

Why Lox?

The word *lox* comes directly from *Lachs*, German for salmon. The term *lox* when it stands by itself (and this is a word that has been corrupted over time) refers to salmon placed in salt brine and smoked, the traditional pushcart fish from the turn of the twentieth century.

The term *nova* or *nova lox* originated because Eastern European Jews in the United States purchased lox from Nova Scotia, which resulted in the abbreviation. Finally, belly lox is salmon that has been cured in brine but not smoked. Belly lox is more tender and flavorful and also more expensive.

The ubiquitous salted or cured or smoked salmon appears as the perfect complement to bagels and cream cheese. The salmon comes from many parts of the world. You can buy Gaspé nova from Canada, Western nova from the Pacific, and Baltic, Scottish, Irish, and Norwegian salmon. But very little salmon comes from Nova Scotia today.

Bagel, Last Words

Who knew when that seventeenth-century Viennese baker honored King Jan with a stirrup-shaped *Bügel* it would achieve such universal popularity in the United States? Most of those early consumers of the bagel—when it was plain and poppy seed—could never imagine that one day varieties would include raisin, chocolate chip, sun-dried tomato, and other regional American concoctions. Can the salsa or the jalapeño bagel be far behind? Maybe they're already here.

In any case, the bagel is a wonderful way to eat anything. At only 200 calories, it's great for kids and adults.

The Carnegie Deli offers a delicious smoked nova, onions, and scrambled egg dish served with a toasted bagel, of course.

(See the next page for Bob Orzo's suggestions for making the perfect bagel, lox, and cream cheese sandwich.)

Annie Smith, Waitress: "Attack of the Decaf Gotchas"

Annie Smith looks like the friendliest grandmother at a PTA cake and cookie sale. She's petite and manages to have a big smile on her face always.

BAGEL, LOX, AND CREAM CHEESE
(Serves One)

This is Bob Orzo's preference for making a toasted bagel, lox, and cream cheese sandwich at home.

Ingredients

1 beefsteak tomato
1 red onion
2 ounces cream cheese
2 ounces lox
1 fresh bagel (purchased not more than four hours after being made)
Capers

Instructions

1. Slice the tomato into thin slices.
2. Slice the red onion into thin slices.
3. Slice the bagel in half and set it under the broiler. (*Not the toaster!*) Flame broil the two open sides until they are nicely brown. (*Don't take your eyes off the bagel or you will have a burned bagel.*)
4. Remove the bagel from the broiler.
5. Spread the cream cheese evenly over the bagel.
6. Layer on the tomato and onion.
7. Add the lox and sprinkle with a few capers.

To Serve

Some people like to make a sandwich; others like to eat one side at a time. Others like to eat it with a knife and fork. Bob recommends using 3 ounces of cream cheese if you're not serving lox.

She started waiting on tables at the Carnegie Deli 16 years ago, having previously worked at the once-popular Columbia Coffee Shop located in the Americana Hotel.

Asked why she came to the Carnegie Deli, she replied truthfully, "I knew there was good business here. You follow the money."

Two years ago, this unassuming and pleasant server was thrust into the network television spotlight in the most unusual of quasi-journalistic faux exposés: She had committed the dastardly deed, the unconscionable act, the almost unmentionable commission of mixing in a wee dram of caffeinated coffee in a decaffeinated order. And this supposedly horrifying act was videotaped and later verified by laboratory analysis.

A television program that seemingly had nothing more interesting to report on a slow news day decided to see whether an order of decaf coffee at New York restaurants actually produced the desired decaf cup. A team of spying reporters visited different restaurants, ordering decaf, which they clandestinely poured into small, hidden cups to be taken back to the lab.

One day, the decaf posse rode into the Carnegie Deli. Some of the undercover reporters sat at Annie Smith's tables. They ordered decaf and then ordered more decaf; nothing could quench their passion for decaf coffee. The demand for decaf resulted in an accelerated decrease of the brewed supply.

She topped off one cup of decaf with a small drop of real coffee. When a reporter set her up with the pointed question of whether caffeinated coffee was ever poured purposely or accidentally into a decaf cup, Annie responded declaratively, "Here at the Carnegie, we never make a mistake." These words were secretly recorded.

The subsequent analysis indicated with precise chemical affirmation that caffeinated coffee had been served in a decaf order.

Then, the television crew returned with the proof of the deception and, in harsh tones more associated with the gotcha revelations of exposed scam or bunco artists, pointed the accusatory finger at little Annie Smith. "What happens if a customer can't drink caffeinated coffee?" shouted one reporter.

The before-and-after Carnegie Deli episodes were aired on television. The waitress in this scarlet affair was the unnamed Annie Smith of Queens, New York.

The day after the broadcast, she was recognized everywhere by friends and neighbors. Suddenly, people she didn't know shouted, "Hi, Annie." She had become a minicelebrity. She was embarrassed by the newfound fame and did not want to return to work. But Sandy Levine insisted that she do the regular shift as though nothing had happened.

The notoriety bothered Annie until people coming to eat at the Carnegie Deli wanted to sit at the table of the nice, friendly, and grandmotherly waitress who poured the coffee.

"After I was on television, my tips increased," she said.

COURSE
5

JACK SIROTA, WAITER: "LAST OF THE ORIGINALS"

Jack Sirota is the last of a now-forgotten breed, the disrespectful but humorous, professional delicatessen waiter. He has been plying his trade and shtick for more than 50 years and is the memory link back to waiting tables in the Catskills. He is also the connection back to the management of the Carnegie Deli from the Max Hudes era to the Steiner-Parker partnership, and up to the present day of Sandy Levine management.

Since 1959, he has been a waiter at the Carnegie Deli, accumulating more stories about the restaurant and the celebrities than anyone else. Semi-retired now, he still comes in for a guest appearance for a photo shoot or to share his recollections about the good old days. As the Carnegie succeeded over time, so did Jack's prominence; he became one of the most well known of the staff—quoted and photographed often.

His tale begins in 1951 at the Neville, a resort in the Catskills at a time when most of New York City's Jewish population vacationed in these New York State mountains.

It was a girlfriend that first attracted Sirota to the Catskills. After three months of summer work, he came back to New York and worked a bread and cake route in Brooklyn. The call of the Catskills was powerful, and Sirota returned a year later to begin a five-year stint as a full-time waiter at the Avon Lodge.

Sirota recalled this Avon Lodge experience as "the best time in my life. I was a king. I made a good living. I met wonderful show business celebrities. I had a new car, I hunted and fished in the seasons, and I dated a few nice gals also."

At the Avon Lodge, Sirota discovered that waiting on 10 people for a week or a month allowed him to get to know the customers. The better he knew their preferences and quirks, the easier it was to provide better service. And better service resulted in higher tips.

For Sirota, the Lodge's most memorable guest during these years was Sid Caesar, the television host of the popular *Your Show of Shows*. Caesar would unwind at the Avon Lodge in the off-season, coming with two brothers for some pinochle and some shooting. The Avon Lodge built a huge hill of dirt to let Caesar fire a .357 Magnum at empty halvah cans filled with water and also a line of cans of unopened shaving cream.

Later in the week, the wives would come to the Lodge. In those days, Caesar was a *shtarker* (Yiddish for a virile, robust man), powerfully built with a big appetite. He would feast on two dishes that have almost vanished from the delicatessen and restaurant world: *cholent* and *p'cha*. *Cholent* is a slow-cooked stew made with lima or navy beans, boiled beef or brisket, and vegetables. *P'cha* is calf's foot jelly, a great favorite of Russian and Polish Jews, made with large amounts of garlic to give the gelatinous dish a pungent taste.

In 1959, Sirota returned to New York to marry Rene, and the couple celebrated 45 married years in 2004. They have one daughter, Susan Jean.

Sirota found a job at Reuben's on East 58th Street. The landmark Manhattan delicatessen restaurant was known for its turf cheesecake. It is also regarded as the originator of the reuben sandwich, created by Arnold Reuben. It was said that he made the sandwich in 1914 to feed Annette Seelos, Charlie Chaplin's leading lady. It included meat, cheese, coleslaw, and Russian dressing on buttered toasted rye.

COME TO THE CARNEGIE

Sirota had to wear a tuxedo at Reuben's and longed for a more casual ambience. A friend told him about the Carnegie Deli, and he served a trial shift one Sunday night, making a third less in tips than at Reuben's. At the Carnegie that evening, he earned $17.20, receiving two one-dollar bills, and the rest in change. Sirota said he tilted like a mailman with a full letter bag from the heavy change.

Max Hudes liked Sirota's work; he was a trained professional who demonstrated an easy, bantering style with the customers. When business at Reuben's fell off, Sirota came over full-time to the Carnegie, which had another advantage—a free parking space on West 55th Street when he drove up for the night shift.

In the years from 1959 to the end of the Max Hudes era in 1976, Sirota described the Carnegie Deli as an unpretentious place where locals came to enjoy a good delicatessen meal. He also remembered many South American Jewish businessmen who showed up for old-style Eastern European cooking that they could not find in Caracas or Buenos Aires.

Sirota praised Max Hudes and his partners. He said, "They never missed a payroll in the many years I worked there."

ENTER STEINER AND PARKER

The first inkling for Sirota that the new Carnegie Deli would be different from the old came when Steiner started to cure meats by hand in the basement. Max Hudes had bought meats from a wholesaler as did other delis in Manhattan. The second event was the considerable increase in the size of the sandwiches, which went from four ounces to eight ounces. Steiner instructed the waiters to put out a free bowl of sour pickles, sour tomatoes, and peppers.

Sirota worked with Leo Steiner for 11 years. He said, "Leo gave from his heart. He also gave from the counter and the kitchen. It was his idea to make a good VIP customer by offering the first meal free. He also paid the checks of many celebrities and any person he thought was important to the deli like bankers."

CELEBRITY SERVING

In 45 years of waiting tables at the Carnegie Deli, Jack Sirota has served the high and the mighty. Here are some short anecdotal riffs about some of the many celebrities:

- *Peter Falk.* In the early 1960s, the actor was a Carnegie regular who ordered beef and stuffed cabbage. He dropped his wallet with $40 left inside. Sirota found it, and Falk tipped him $4, saying, "That's all I can afford." (This was years before his success in *Columbo.*)
- *The Famous Writers' Group.* This consisted of Paddy Chayefsky (*Marty*), Herb Gardner (*A Thousand Clowns*), and Noel Behn (*The Brink's Job*), and also Broadway and film director Bob Fosse (*Sweet Charity*). They discussed projects and the theater every day.

- *Mel Allen.* The radio and television voice of the New York Yankees was born in Birmingham, Alabama, as Mel Allen Israel. "He became Jewish again when he entered the Carnegie," said Sirota. "He ordered chicken in the pot and said it was just like his mother made."
- *Maria Von Trapp.* A steady customer, beautifully dressed, almost six feet tall. She always ordered the nova lox plate.
- *Henny Youngman.* "Henny said to me, 'Jack, I tip the same to everyone, here at the Carnegie Deli or at the Friars Club.' I told him, 'Henny, you're a lousy tipper at the Friars and a lousy tipper here at the Carnegie.'"
- *Rick Pitino.* "When he was coaching basketball at Kentucky, he brought in the entire team when they were visiting New York. These kids' eyes popped out when they saw the size of the sandwiches."
- *Don King.* Sirota rated him the best customer. He comes in with two or three friends, says hello to the staff, and tips $50 to $100.
- *Mr. T.* Another favorite customer. Outgoing and gregarious. Happy to accommodate the autograph seekers. He also makes friends with children. Once, he showed up in an open horse and buggy.
- *Anne Meara and Jerry Stiller.* Sirota said, "They're like family to me. They ask for my table each time they come in." Their daughter has the same birthday as Sirota's.

Sirota also recalled one of the most delightful afternoons when the Marimba Band of Japan comprised of young Japanese children stopped in after a concert at Carnegie Hall. They gave Sirota a souvenir kimono.

Here are some interesting stories from the not-so-famous diners:

- *The man from Mattel.* An executive from Mattel gave Sirota a Barbie doll in its box for a tip. It was the first doll in his daughter's Barbie doll collection and one of the most valuable.
- *The professional gambler.* On Fridays at 3 P.M., a professional gambler used to come in with a bodyguard. Once, when he could not come in, he sent the bodyguard with Sirota's tip and an apology for missing the usual afternoon meal.
- *Shady businessmen.* One notorious swindler used to come in and order two steaks and broccoli and leave Sirota a $20 tip. He kept a suite in every hotel to avoid being discovered by his wife when he was on the town with his mistress. Another shyster dined daily on one Danish and coffee. He paid with a hundred-dollar bill to launder illegal cash payoffs and pocketed the change.
- *The everyday diners.* A man ate blintzes every week for 30 years. A woman, who ate in the Carnegie Deli daily, always ordered a baked potato with butter and two Ballantine ales.
- *The horse owner.* He left Sirota a $50 betting ticket on a trotter horse running at Roosevelt Race Track. The horse won at very short odds of two to five, and Sirota collected an additional $20 for a total of $70. Not a bad tip.

THE LIFE OF THE WAITER

Sirota has enjoyed waiting on tables, and he relished the many years at the Carnegie. He said, "I've been 100 percent for the store. I bent over backwards to help the Carnegie. Here everyone helps out everyone else." He believed that in order to provide the best service, a waiter has to develop a quick rapport with a customer. Often, it's a simple act, like bringing extra bread along with the big sandwiches, or filling up the free bowl of pickles and sour tomatoes.

After more than 50 years working the floor, he believed that there was no foolproof method to tell who will be a good tipper or who will not. One approach he has used has been to wait on a single person whom other waiters rejected since the tab would be low and so would the subsequent gratuity. He has also volunteered to wait on difficult customers when other waiters begged off or when coworkers were in a bad mood.

He has enjoyed bantering with the Carnegie's customers, but he preferred out-of-towners who came for the food and for a taste of that old-time New York deli shtick. Sometimes, though, the introductory waiter act met with surprising results. One rushed customer said, "Pastrami sandwich now and schmoozing later."

His answer to the snobby know-nothings who demanded a "lean pastrami" was, "It's trimmed beforehand. We don't sell fat here."

Sirota experienced a few Carnegie coincidences. The girl he went to visit in the Catskills in 1951 came in as a customer in 1982. At a wedding, he was introduced to a couple who "owned the Carnegie Deli." This seemed odd to him because he did not recognize Max Hudes or Milton Parker and their wives. The couple turned out to be Ida and Izzie Orgel, the original owners who founded the Carnegie Deli in 1937.

Sirota has been featured in GQ magazine. He is one of the two remaining Jewish waiters still serving at the Carnegie Deli. He still remembers that a three-ounce pastrami sandwich was 60 cents in 1960.

Asked what makes a good customer, he replied, "A good customer knows what to tip and is in and out of the Carnegie in 20 minutes."

RASMEE RUENANUKOOL, WAITRESS: "LADY OF SMILES"

Rasmee originally comes from Thailand and has been a permanent waitress at the Carnegie Deli for 19 years, which makes her one of the first Asian women to be a server. After a brief stint at Orloff's deli restaurant on Broadway, she then worked at the Stage Delicatessen. However, on her walks from the subway to the Stage, she noticed the fast-moving lines in front of the Carnegie Deli. She applied for a tough-to-get server's job. Her work experience at the two other delis convinced Leo Steiner to hire her.

In the beginning, she had to prove that she could serve deli, particularly to the satisfaction of the old-time male waiters who had doubts that a petite, smiling Asian-American woman could work the hectic Carnegie Deli. Also, some customers back then wanted to sit at a "Jewish" waiter's table to participate in what they perceived was the authentic New York deli experience.

Today, the clientele is happy to sit at any table served by the multinational serving staff.

Rasmee's most memorable Carnegie Deli customer was former Vice President Al Gore. She always feels excited when a new celebrity comes in. But everyone gets the same good service and the wonderful smile.

Her Thai friends occasionally stop in at the restaurant and order pastrami, which has enough spices to please their spicy palates. She brings in her own Thai soup because nothing at the Carnegie tastes like the homemade dish.

She said, "Everyone likes working here. It's like family."

Muriel Caraballo, Waitress: "CBS NFL Warm-Up"

Muriel started out in the Carnegie Deli as a waitress in 1991. She worked at different Manhattan restaurants for 20 years, but always wanted to come to the Carnegie Deli. Her chance arrived when her friend Mary, another waitress at the deli, tipped her off to the opening of the deli's back room.

She has observed the many customers who have come in to dine and has stated that resident New Yorkers bring in business associates and friends from out of town more frequently than coming in by themselves. "They like to show off the Carnegie as a special, one-of-a-kind, New York place," she said.

Muriel praised tour guides and the many hotels in the area for their instructional advice to tourists—but above all, to foreigners—about the standard tipping practices for restaurants in New York. Over time, she witnessed that very few foreign visitors fail to leave the minimum 15 percent gratuity. Many foreign visitors showed her guidebooks written in their native languages, which admonished the reader to leave a proper tip in New York, warning that an irate server might follow the customer out to the street, shouting and waving the check!

She has often waited on celebrities and chided a famous singer (name not revealed) for being snooty and pulling a Greta Garbo "I want to be alone" routine with the staff. The opposite example is Sylvester Stallone, who comes in with a retinue of people. In one sense, he is not approachable by customers seeking autographs, but he always acts pleasantly to the staff.

Muriel's advice to celebrities is, "If you don't want to be noticed, don't come to the Carnegie Deli."

One of her favorite celebrity customers is boxing promoter Don King. He comes in with a big hello to the staff and often picks up the check for diners at the next table.

For the past eight years, she has worked Sunday mornings and is the waitress of choice for the on-air personnel of CBS's popular Sunday television pregame sports show, *The NFL Today*. The CBS studios are two blocks away. Broadcasters Jim Nantz and Pat Leahy were the first to come in on a regular basis for the traditional Carnegie Deli breakfast. Then, as new announcer Dan Marino joined the team, he also accompanied the regulars for breakfast.

Muriel considered the broadcast crew as part of her Sunday morning family. She said, "They're all gentlemen and very easy to serve. When the last NFL game is aired in the winter, they say to me, 'Muriel, see you next week.' But I know I won't see them again until the NFL show comes on again in September."

Meats of the Deli World

The beef that ends up in the sandwiches and on the plates of a delicatessen starts out as cuts from the shoulder, breast, and flank. The main types of meat served in a deli—brisket, flanken, corned beef, tongue, and pastrami—require either long-time cooking or specialized curing to bring out the flavor from these less-tender cuts.

Brisket

When cooked well, this is as tasty a meat cut as comes from the cow. Brisket requires hours of cooking, and sometimes it shrinks considerably in size. It is sold boneless and in two parts, and cooks often buy double portions to feed four or six diners.

The sauce that covers the brisket adds immeasurably to the flavor of the stringy but tender meat. Recently, friends tasted a brisket that had diced kumquat and chutney added to the sauce for extra flavoring.

Cooks in the North and Midwest use brisket as the base for corned beef. But Southerners and Southwesterners often barbecue this cut. The stringy meat takes to marinating and also to slathering gobs of tangy barbecue sauce on top. When grilled, the meat pulls apart easily, so the flavorful strands can be placed inside hot dog rolls or hamburger buns or on top of bread. The name derives from the Old English.

Flanken

This cut enjoys many different names: short ribs, braised ribs, or chuck short ribs. The cuts are rectangular with the option of leaving the bone in or having it removed. Short ribs are tough and packed with meaty fat, which is the main reason why they are braised or boiled.

Delis serve boiled flanken, an entree that is gradually diminishing in popularity. It's a hearty, filling dish on a cold day. The Carnegie Deli entree recipe for boiled flanken is on page 116.

The word comes from the Yiddish, plural of *flanke*, meaning flank or side, and from the French *flanc*.

Corned Beef

People are surprised that corn has nothing to do with this tasty meat. *Corn* is an Anglo-Saxon terminology for coarse salt, sometimes so large that the granules or pellets resembled kernels of coarse grain. In this instance, corned is the past tense of the verb "to corn."

Corned beef starts out at the Carnegie Deli commissary as full-cut shoulder briskets, weighing 15 to 17 pounds. The brisket is taken to an automated machine and given an abundant infusion of a brine solution. Then, it is placed in a brine-filled barrel and refrigerated for an additional week.

The final step is to boil the corned beef for three and a half to four and a half hours at the Carnegie Deli. Then, it is brought immediately to the counter. All the fat is trimmed, and the corned beef is sliced and piled up to five delicious inches atop rye bread.

The commissary also packs the quick-chilled corned beef in air-free plastic containers to ship to food distributors throughout the United States. The corned beef you eat at a restaurant, hotel, or country club in El Rancho Poway Grande or Haddonfield may be the authentic Carnegie Deli brand (and it can be advertised on the menu if it is).

What to do with those corned beef leftovers? Make corned beef hash by following the Carnegie Deli's recipe on page 117.

Tongue

Tongue is a delicacy, but it is not for every palate. Some cooks bake tongue in the same manner as brisket, but the difference is that the flavor of tongue is enhanced by adding ginger, cloves, bay leaves, brown sugar, nutmeg, and paprika. It is served hot and sliced with mustard or horseradish.

The most famous tongue sandwich was the Dagwood, introduced in 1936 by cartoonist Chuck Young and featured in the comic strip *Blondie*. The first Dagwood sandwich consisted of tongue, onion, mustard, sardines, beans, and horseradish.

At the commissary, the tongue arrives from the highest quality U.S. meat packers. It is also given a brine injection to add flavor to the meat. It is placed next in a brine solution and cured for a week before it makes the trip to the Carnegie Deli, where it is boiled before being served. A tongue sandwich ranks third in popularity at the Carnegie.

Pastrami

Pastrami is the undisputed king of Jewish deli meats. According to comedian Jackie Mason, in an interview in New York's *Newsday* magazine, "I feel pastrami is the most tasty thing that was ever invented."

History

The history of the name has two possible routes: The first is the Turkish *basturma* that became *pastirma*, and the second is the Yiddish *pastrame*, from the Romanian *pastramă*.

If you follow the Turkish semantic trail, you begin with horsemen riding the steppes of Central Asia, their salted or pressed meat nestled in their saddles. When the nomadic Turks (who came originally from Central Asia) settled in Turkey, they began to domesticate the preparation of cured meats. Today, the *pastrima* is a Turkish national dish, cured with salt and an array of locally ground spices called *çemen* and then air-dried outside in the warm sun.

Keep to the Yiddish-Romanian (the latter language is a Latin derivative) past and you go further back in time to the Vulgar Latin verb *parsitāre*, which means "to spare or to save." In effect, pastrami is a verb used for curing or seasoning.

The Commissary Preparation

The mouth-watering pastrami from the Carnegie Deli begins as a four-to-six-pound navel from the steer's fourth rib area. (The commissary goes through so many navels that it must use many meat suppliers, since no one meat packer can supply the extraordinary number of navels destined to become five tons of weekly pastrami.)

The navels are sent to the automated brine machine where they are given a healthy injection, flooding the meat with the solution. They are placed in brine and spice-filled barrels and cured for a week.

After the one-week brine bath, the navels are coated with a special, course rub of caramel, coriander, pepper, paprika, and other seasonings (remember the spicy Turkish *çemen* coating). The coated navels are hung on smokehouse trees (racks). Then, these are smoked for up to five hours with hickory chip smoke, which adds more taste.

What starts out as a coated navel comes out as pastrami. After smoking, the pastramis are quick-chilled and packed for shipment to the Carnegie Deli early in the morning, and they are also sent (like the corned beef) to food distributors nationwide.

Back at the Carnegie Deli, the pastramis are placed in the steam table and steamed for three and a half to four and a half hours. The fat is left on the meat to keep the flavor in and to provide moisture. After the steaming, all the fat is cut off the pastrami.

Ordering a Pastrami Sandwich at the Deli

Pastrami has its own ordering nickname, "a pistol." At the Carnegie Deli, you will hear the servers calling out, "A pistol on whiskey down" (rye bread toasted) or "A pistol dressed" (Russian dressing and coleslaw on the bread).

The reason is not because pastrami is the king of sandwiches and merits its own special name. You be the counterman for a moment. What would you make if you heard a server shout, "Ordering a . . . *ami* on rye to go." Did you answer, "pastrami"? Or on second thought, do you think it was "salami"? When you hear the words pistol or salami, there's never any confusion.

What to do with those pastrami sandwich leftovers? Make pastrami hash with the Carnegie Deli's recipe on page 117.

NEED A PASTRAMI, CORNED BEEF, OR TONGUE SANDWICH FIX?

Can't buy it where you live? Check the Carnegie Deli's menu on-line at www.carnegiedeli.com. Then, call the Carnegie Deli's take-out line and a delicious package will be sent to you via FedEx the next day. The number is (800) 334-5606. Pickles and mustard are included. But you knew that.

ENTREE RECIPES

BEEF FLANKEN
(Serves Four to Six)

This is a wonderful recipe from the Old World cooking tradition. It takes a little time to make, but not a lot of elaborate preparation.

Ingredients

4 pounds short ribs
2 carrots, peeled
2 cups green onions, chopped
½ cup celery, chopped
4 cups beef stock
Salt and pepper to taste
6 medium white potatoes

Instructions

1. Place short ribs, carrots, onion, and celery in a pot. Cover with stock. Add salt and pepper to taste.
2. Boil for 2 to 3 hours, then let cool for 5 minutes.
3. Boil potatoes and keep warm until serving.
4. Remove all bones from the meat.

To Serve

Place a portion of meat in the center of each plate and surround the meat with the vegetables and the potatoes. Add a sprig of parsley.

Corned Beef or Pastrami Hash
(Serves Two)

Many Carnegie Deli diners take home wrapped pastrami or corned beef and refrigerate it for later use. This is a tasty recipe for taking the extra meat that you could not finish at the deli and whipping up an appetizing, hot meal for breakfast, lunch, or dinner.

Ingredients

Pastrami or corned beef cut into small squares
1 green pepper, diced
1 medium white onion, diced
1 medium white potato, peeled and boiled
Olive oil
Salt and pepper to taste
Paprika

Instructions

1. Sauté the pepper, onion, and potato in olive oil in a skillet over medium heat.
2. Let the vegetables and potato cook until the onion is wilted.
3. Add salt and pepper, and some paprika for color (but not too much).
4. Drop in the pastrami or corned beef and mix with the vegetables.
5. Cook for 3 or 4 minutes, stirring.

To Serve

For breakfast, you can make eggs to go with the hash. Some people will want ketchup or steak sauce for the hash. Serve with toasted rye bread.

Chicken Consommé and Chicken in the Pot
(Serves One)

Old-timers remember with fondness from their deli dining experience the tasty chicken in the pot.

Consommé Ingredients

1 pound chicken, cut up
½ ounce chicken base
1 celery stalk
1 small white onion
Salt and pepper to taste

Consommé Instructions

Boil the previous ingredients in ½ gallon of water for an hour.

Ingredients for Chicken in the Pot

½ fresh chicken, cut into 4 pieces
1 cup chicken consommé
1 carrot, peeled and cut into 1-inch lengths
1 celery stalk, cut into ½-inch lengths
Salt and pepper to taste

Instructions for Chicken in the Pot

1. Place the pieces of chicken (with or without the skin) into a pot.
2. Cover the chicken with the consommé.
3. Add the carrot and celery and season to taste.
4. Boil for 20 to 25 minutes.

To Serve

Serve on a dinner plate with a boiled potato.

CHICKEN PAPRIKASH CASSEROLE
(Serves One)

Here's a tasty change of pace for the chicken lover who wants a zesty bird served in a delicious sauce. Close your eyes and be transported back to Old Budapest.

Ingredients

½ roasting chicken, cut into small pieces
1 medium white onion, chopped
1 green pepper, diced
1 can tomato sauce
2 teaspoons paprika
½ cup white rice
Salt and pepper to taste

Instructions

1. In a large bowl, mix the pieces of chicken with the onion, pepper, tomato sauce, paprika, and seasoning.
2. Bake in a covered pot for 45 minutes at 350 degrees.
3. Cook the rice until fluffy.

To Serve

Pour the chicken and sauce over the rice. The chicken paprika casserole is the only Carnegie Deli entree that is served on a bed of rice.

Stuffed Cabbage
(Serves Two)

Cabbage is a multipurpose vegetable that is a staple of the world's cuisines. In delis, stuffed cabbage has been a delicious treat for years.

Ingredients

1 head green cabbage (center core removed)
1 pound chopped beef
½ cup bread crumbs
1 green onion, chopped
½ teaspoon garlic, minced
2 eggs
1 cup tomato sauce—see recipe below
1 cup white rice
1 tablespoon brown sugar
Salt and pepper to taste

Instructions

1. Boil the cabbage leaves in a pot of water for about 5 minutes.
2. Mix together meat, bread crumbs, onion, garlic, eggs, rice, salt, and pepper.
3. Roll the meat mixture into the cabbage leaves.
4. *Sauce:* Take four chopped cabbage leaves, and boil with 1 tablespoon brown sugar, salt, and 1 cup of canned tomatoes.
5. Place rolled cabbage leaves in a pot, pour the tomato sauce over them, cover, and bake at 350 degrees for an hour.
6. Serve (or cover and refrigerate for later use).

To Serve

Two pieces can be served with a boiled potato and other vegetables as a main dish. For an appetizer, serve one piece.

BRISKET OF BEEF
(Serves Six to Eight)

Brisket represented the culinary heights for mothers in the Old Country. No one in the *shtetls* could afford the more expensive sirloin and tenderloin cuts. The meat was tough and fatty, and required long hours to cook, plus it often needed a savory sauce.

Ingredients

8 pounds brisket of beef
4 cloves garlic
4 cups chicken broth or consommé
Salt and pepper to taste
6 green onions, sliced into ½-inch pieces
1 celery stalk
4 carrots, sliced into ½-inch pieces
12 large white potatoes, peeled and quartered

Instructions

1. Preheat oven to 350 degrees.
2. Place brisket in roasting pan and cover with chicken broth.
3. Season liberally with salt, pepper, and garlic.
4. Place onions, celery, and carrots both on the top and alongside the brisket. Add the potatoes on the side.
5. Cover the roasting pan with tinfoil and roast for 3 hours until meat is tender.
6. Roast for an additional 30 minutes uncovered to brown the brisket.

To Serve

Serve on a large platter with the sliced meat on one side and the vegetables on the other.

2004: PICKLE-EATING CONTEST

Every two years, during the third week in May, the Carnegie Deli and its sole pickle supplier, United Pickle of the Bronx, New York, conduct a pickle-eating contest at the restaurant.

In 2004, 10 contestants vied for who could eat the most sour pickles in a five-minute period. The winner was Cookie Jarvis, who downed three pounds, beating out by a pickle end second-place finisher Arnie Chapman, who ate 2.9 pounds. Nineteen pounds of pickles were crunched on that day.

In 2004, United Pickle marked its 107th year in business. The Leibowitz family has always owned the company, and it is the last of the large New York City-area pickle suppliers, which once totaled as many as 200 in the 1950s.

The company specializes in the "New York taste," says owner Steve Leibowitz. It makes fresh, refrigerated pickles without vinegar and sells to delicatessens and food distributing companies. Steve's son runs the famous Gus's Pickles.

Pickles have been eaten for more than 4,000 years. Explorer Amerigo Vespucci started out as a supplier of pickles. He found they were a way to ward off scurvy on his ships. In fact, pickles are a good source of vitamin C. Americans eat more than 20 million pickles a year.

Two bad pickle jokes: What is a pickle? A cucumber turned sour after a *jarring* experience. And, What is a pickle lover's favorite television game show? It's *Let's Make a Dill*.

In 2006, during May's annual International Pickle Week, the Carnegie and United Pickle will conduct the next pickle-eating contest. Mark it on your calendar.

SANDY LEVINE, MANAGING DIRECTOR OF RETAIL AND MBD: "THE HAPPY DELI MAN"

I n the mid-1990s, Jeff Jensen traveled with Sandy Levine to a meeting in Washington, DC. The team planned to discuss a possible wholesale cheesecake business with the executives of the well-known Palm Restaurant chain.

Jensen delivered a slide presentation on the operation of the Carnegie Deli's commissary. From time to time, he nodded in Levine's direction and said, "Sandy is the Carnegie Deli's managing director of retail and MBD," or, "I always check in first with our resident MBD." At the end of the presentation, Jensen turned the meeting over to questions from the floor, knowing that the first one from any Palm executive would be (as it was), "What does *MBD* mean?"

Then Jensen delivered the punch line, "MBD means Married Boss's Daughter." The meeting burst into gales of laughter. The president of the Palm organization was pleased, announcing, "I'm the Palm's MBD, but I never knew how to introduce myself."

Today, Levine's business card reads, *Sanford Levine, MBD*. It is a tribute to his good nature and fine sense of humor that he placed the initials on the business card. It's on the web site, also.

Sandy Levine represented the final step in the continuation of the efficient management and high quality of the Carnegie Deli. He arrived at the deli in 1992, a time when his father-in-law, Milton Parker, started to bring to an end the satellite Carnegies that had never reached the profit potential everyone had anticipated. It was also the time when the commissary began to explore outside wholesale accounts.

As history would prove many years later, Sandy was the right man for the right job at the right time. But no one knew that fact in 1992 because Sandy Levine did not have one hour of food or restaurant or deli experience. In fact, this Brooklyn, New York, native had never before tasted a Carnegie Deli pastrami sandwich. "Eating at the Carnegie Deli was too rich for my tastes. I ate deli locally," he said.

Bring in the Civilian

Sandy Levine worked for years in the clothing business as a buyer for shops and discount department stores. He married and divorced and has two grown daughters, Cari and Jodi. He met his wife Marian, who was also divorced with a nine-year-old daughter, Sarri, at Bob Fosse's restaurant The Laundry on Long Island. The couple clicked and, after a brief courtship, married in 1991.

By 1991, Milton Parker was 72. He had managed the deli single-handedly with different managers for the four years after Steiner's death. He wanted to keep the profitable Carnegie

Deli in the family. Parker sought Marian's advice: Could his new son-in-law learn and then lead the business?

The conversations continued over time. Marian emphasized that Sandy had an outgoing extrovertish personality, and he was good with people. He was accustomed to getting up early in the morning and working long hours in the day.

Milton Parker realized that Sandy's time was running out as the head the import-export clothing firm. The owners had younger sons who would soon take over the family-owned operation. Parker offered Sandy a job at the deli at double his salary and Sandy accepted.

Parker organized a series of on-the-job training sessions, some of which lasted for weeks and months. The new hire opened the deli at 6 A.M., working with the cooks to prepare the restaurant for breakfast. He worked with the countermen at lunch, making the big sandwiches and learning the deli lingo for "pistol and CB." He stayed nights, watching the evening cooks prepare flanken and stuffed cabbage.

Sandy checked the inventory system in the basement. He did the payroll and interfaced with the unions. He spent lots of time with Jeff Jensen in the New Jersey commissary. He checked the bathrooms, listened to the employees' complaints and suggestions, did the ordering and met the suppliers, took constructive criticism from his father-in-law, and shared the daily deli experiences with his wife.

After years of training, Levine started to feel comfortable making decisions. But, in truth, the training program lasted 10 years, or until 2002 when Milton Parker gave up running the daily operation. The instructions from Parker to his son-in-law were always clear: Learn the deli business the Carnegie Deli way.

Sandy has always appreciated Parker's presence in the deli. He said, "I'm a quick learner and I'm still learning. Milton has been in the business for years, and he always knows what's best for the deli. I only tried to follow his example."

Everyone who works at the Carnegie will acknowledge that the one area of the business that is quintessentially Sandy and unlearned from any training program is schmoozing with the customers. The jovial Sandy is part maitre d', part *tummler* (what the social director of a Catskills hotel was called), part greeter, part New York City booster, part complaint department, part matchmaker, while keeping up a steady pace of cheerful chatter.

Sandy as the Managing Director

Parker introduced Sandy to the media because he knew from years of experience that television, newspapers, and magazines would continue to come to the Carnegie for stories and anecdotes. He wanted to have Sandy with his sunny personality act as the spokesperson for the deli.

After the first three years in training, Sandy began to grasp the basics of the Carnegie Deli. He began to take charge of the day-to-day operation. He noticed that many of the staff started to come to him for instructions.

In the beginning, Sandy did what any savvy executive does with a well-run and profitable business: He made no drastic changes. He said, "It's a cliché, but if it's not broke, don't fix it."

From the years of working in the clothing business, Sandy learned the lesson that employee morale and loyalty were always higher when the staff knew that hard work and dedication would result in a promotion. He said, "I have one major principle when it comes to the people who work at the deli: I always promote from within. I do not hire staff from the outside. I would need to train them the Carnegie way, which would be a waste of time. The current Carnegie employee knows the system. All of our countermen and cooks started out on the bottom rung."

When he felt comfortable, Sandy implemented a change that startled and pleased everyone. He made the sandwiches even bigger! How high the sandwich sky? Sandy noticed that other New York delis had increased the size of their sandwiches, and he wanted to make certain that the Carnegie maintained its weight and height supremacy. A combo like the Broadway Danny Rose tops over eight inches and contains 1½ pounds of meat.

The *New York Daily News* published an article in its Tuesday Now section of April 5, 2003, listing the tallest pastrami sandwich in the metropolitan area. The winner and still champ was the Carnegie Deli, which measured 4½ to 5 inches tall. Piled high at the deli means a full pound of delicious cured meats. The combo sandwiches go higher and seem to defy gravity, rising to a height of almost eight inches.

The Carnegie's generous portions have given rise to the two most famous of the Sandyisms, the oft-quoted deli managing director's witty remarks: "If you finish your meal at the Carnegie, we've made a mistake." And "If you can put your mouth around the Carnegie combo sandwich, we haven't put on enough meat."

THE SANDY SYSTEM

During the decade of the 1990s, tourists dominated the Carnegie Deli's business, and today they represent more than 95 percent of customers on any given day. The deli has become a "must stop" on the "must see" list of sights and tastes of Manhattan. Many locals also enjoy the delicatessen fare by making stops for lunch or dinner, or by ordering takeout for delivery to their offices and homes.

Sandy boasts to natives and visitors alike, "Once you've eaten at the Carnegie, when you go to another deli, you'll know the difference. We're the best."

MEDIA APPEARANCES AND ARTICLES

The Carnegie Deli's first television appearance occurred on CBS's *60 Minutes* in the early 1980s. The late Harry Reasoner did a piece on dining at a famous Swiss restaurant and resort, describing what an exorbitant price a tourist would pay for lunch. The spot ended with a contented Reasoner eating a pastrami sandwich inside the Carnegie Deli and saying, "But *this* is eating."

In the past few years, the Carnegie Deli with Sandy Levine in the starring role has appeared on a number of Food Channel programs. Viewers have learned about the inner workings of the deli and the commissary, and met the waitstaff on *Unwrapped, Into the Fire,* and *Monster Meals.* The well-known Emeril Lagasse invited Sandy to talk about deli on the chef's show *Emeril Live.*

Every year, different media outlets request permission to do an article or an interview. A regional article about the Carlstadt, New Jersey, commissary appeared in the May 10, 2004, edition of *NJBIZ.*

MR. PERSONALITY

Sandy Levine loves what he does. He's on the floor of the Carnegie Deli every morning at 11 o'clock, although his day begins much earlier. He always canvasses the deli in the morning to see that the store is neat and ready for business. It is Sandy's daily walk, and it starts from the front of the dining room and continues to the kitchen, the bathrooms, the back room, and a glance outside to make sure the sidewalk is swept clean.

Many tourists regard the tall (6'1"), balding, happy Sandy Levine as an image from Hollywood's central casting of what a New York deli maven should look and sound like. He seems larger than life and is unafraid to go up to strangers in the deli and ask where they're from or what their plans are while visiting New York. He has a deep voice that can pierce any restaurant din to give an order to a server.

His favorite part of the job is schmoozing with the customers. He listens to what they have to say, always inquiring, "Did you have a good time here?" "Where are you from? I'll bet they don't serve deli like this where you live." And "Did you get enough to eat?"

HE LOVES THE JOB

If you think of the Carnegie Deli as a wonderful cruise ship taking a deli journey, then Sandy Levine is both the captain and the social director. He's in charge of where the ship is going and how it is to be run. He's also chatting with the customers, making sure they're happy, relaxed, and well fed.

When asked about the Carnegie Deli dining experience, Sandy stated, "It's a meeting place. It's a fun place. It's a happy place. And, it's become a vital part of New York deli history."

Sandy is training his son-in-law, Chuck Smith, to manage the Carnegie. The goal is to keep the successful operation in the family.

Sandy is ever conscious that the Carnegie Deli is a business that has to grow. He said, "If you're standing still, you're going behind. I fight for business every day."

MARIAN PARKER LEVINE, DAUGHTER AND WIFE: "ALL IN THE DELI FAMILY"

Marian Parker Levine, Milton's daughter and Sandy's wife, worked in her father's luncheonette as a cashier when she was a teenager. She did not realize that this skill would come in handy at the Carnegie Deli after it opened.

When her father and Leo Steiner took over the restaurant in 1976, the deli's cashier chose not to stay with the new team. The owners were in a tight pinch; they needed someone reliable and trustworthy to work the cash register.

She was 26 and had been educated to teach school. Marian laughed, "My father said to come in for a day or two. I worked there for two years."

Then, the cash register was placed next to the front door. In the wintertime, it was so cold from the wintry blasts coming from the opened door that Marian had to wear warm woolen turtlenecks, scarves, hats, and gloves. She sat in this cold and cramped space next to a chain-smoking woman who answered the phone and shouted or screamed orders to the counterman.

Marian saw that the Carnegie was a place where celebrities congregated. She harbored a secret crush on Barry Manilow and waited for the day when the famous singer would eat lunch at the Carnegie. A year passed and then on that magic day, Barry Manilow came in to eat alone. The waitstaff knew of Marian's crush—she knew his songs by heart—and informed her of his order, which she remembers to this day (triple-decker corned beef and chopped liver on rye—price in 1977? $4.86 with tax).

But Marian could not leave her cashier's station to approach the popular singer. The waiter (who usually took the cash with the check to the cashier) asked Manilow to pay the cashier on the way out as a favor to Marian. Her heart skipped a beat when he approached. She asked for and received his autograph. Today, Barry Manilow's signed picture hangs in the front row of the main dining room section thanks to Marian's insistence on this Carnegie Deli place of honor.

She shared fond memories of Steiner, saying, "Leo was a brilliant food person, dedicated to making everything the best. He was also the guy with the 'Hi, boychick' and interacted with the customers. He also gave away a lot of food. It was his style to be generous and it was smart to give a sample of pastrami to the people outside waiting in line. But he also picked up the tab for a lot of people. After Leo died, when my father stopped the freebies, a lot of the freeloaders never came in again."

Marian remembered the electricity blackout of 1977, the second of the three that have hit New York. She had to crank the cash register manually each time a sale was rung up. She took pride that even in the dark, the amount of money in the register was correct to the penny. She recalled that her father parked his sedan to face inside the deli so that the headlights illuminated the inside of the restaurant.

Marian worked from 8 A.M. to 4 P.M. every day in a stressful restaurant environment. The old-style cash registers did not have the present-day calculator function that indicates the amount of change due. After two years, she became pregnant the week after she quit the cashier's job. Nine months later, her daughter, Sarri, was born.

When her daughter was older, Marian returned to teaching school on Long Island. By 1988, now divorced, she saw an opportunity to return to the Carnegie Deli after Leo Steiner's death. With her father required to be on the floor, she became the back-up businessperson in the office, doing payroll, taxes, and scheduling. Milton and her mother were able to take some vacation time while daughter Marian ran the deli.

The father-and-daughter working together arrangement lasted two years. She quit for a second time.

In 1990, she met Sandy Levine at a restaurant in Easthampton, Long Island. They married soon after. Marian will not say that she thought Sandy could be the new Prince Charming of Pastrami to replace her father running the Carnegie Deli. She stated, "I did not want it because you don't want to let your married life interfere with the family's business."

Fast-forward to many years later when Sandy was in charge of the Carnegie Deli. Marian had a promotional idea: Carnegie Deli T-shirts. She pitched the idea to her husband. He said, "Sure. Let's do it." After 25 years, someone in charge of the Carnegie listened and approved of Marian's terrific promotional idea.

She is the one person at the deli who can sing the verse from Adam Sandler's "The Hanukah Song." "Guess who eats together at the Karnickey Deli, Bowzer from Sha Na Na, and Arthur Fonzerrelli."

When asked about favorite memories of the Carnegie Deli, which has been her home-away-from-home for more than 28 years, she replied, "During one Academy Awards ceremony, I realized that every famous presenter that night had eaten in the Carnegie Deli during the past year.

"We're show business, too."

2004: THE LEVINES' VACATIONS

In 1992, after working day and night for months to learn the delicatessen business, Sandy Levine decided he could steal a few days and take his wife Marian and her daughter Sarri for a short vacation to Disney World in Orlando, Florida.

On a particularly hot day, he wore a Carnegie Deli T-shirt that had just arrived at the restaurant the day before their departure to Florida. At the end of a busy Disney tour, the Levines returned to the hotel. Another vacationing couple entered the elevator at the same time.

"Oh, drat. We missed buying it," said the wife, staring at the T-shirt.

"Missed buying what?" asked Marian, who noticed that the couple's eyes were riveted on the T-shirt that she had designed and ordered.

"We had lunch at the Carnegie Deli two weeks ago. But we did not see the T-shirt. We would have bought one to take home. We won't be back to New York for a long while," the wife lamented.

"They weren't for sale two weeks ago. The shirts arrived last week," answered Marian.

"Hi, I'm Sandy Levine, the managing director of the Carnegie Deli. I'm going to give you this shirt." And he took off the sweaty T-shirt and handed it to the astonished couple.

Marian suggested, "Sandy, why don't you autograph it?"

"Oh, could you, please?" the wife implored.

"With pleasure," said Sandy when Marian handed him a pen.

"Are you really the managing director of the Carnegie Deli?" the man questioned.

Sandy handed the man his business card.

"What does MBD stand for?" the man asked.

"Married Boss's Daughter," Sandy answered.

"I'm the BD," said Marian.

Then the couple praised the delicatessen and thanked the Levines for the generous gesture. They got off the elevator first, flushed with excitement and delighted to possess a genuine Carnegie Deli memento. When the Levines exited on their floor, a woman waiting for the down elevator gave Sandy the disapproving stare of a person horrified to see the naked chest of a perspiring man.

Sandy and Marian Levine

In 2004, Marian and Sandy took a long cruise through the Panama Canal. On board, they were an anonymous couple enjoying the fabulous man-made structure that played such an important part in the late-nineteenth-century history of the United States.

But the master of ceremonies on the boat recognized Sandy, and on the first night in the ballroom said, "Ladies and gentlemen, we have a restaurant celebrity on board. Mr. Sandy Levine of the Carnegie Deli."

The people broke out in spontaneous applause. For the rest of the cruise, almost the entire passenger list shared stories of their past Carnegie Deli visits with the Levines.

Sandy said, "Everyone wanted to talk deli. Deli from their youth and deli eaten in New York."

Marian said, "We had booked this exotic cruise to escape for a few weeks from pastrami and pickles. But once they knew who Sandy was, there was no escape."

JEFF JENSEN, MANAGING DIRECTOR OF WHOLESALE: "MR. CONTENTMENT AT THE COMMISSARY"

For Jeff Jensen, the start of his tenure in the food service business began when his father, Lars, a Danish pastry chef, jumped ship in the 1930s and remained in New York City. On Papa Lars's first visit to America, he stopped at Woolworth's Five and Dime and mistook for diamonds the rhinestones and paste jewelry on the counters.

"My father thought America was the land of opportunity after that," joked Jensen.

Lars Jensen was a master baker who had studied baking in a long and demanding apprenticeship in Denmark. He found work in Manhattan since the skill to prepare and bake breads, cakes, and cookies and make ice cream delicacies in the Old World style was a talent much in demand by higher-class New York restaurants and hotels.

In 1937, Lars began work at the legendary Lindy's restaurant in Manhattan where he improved on the cheesecake recipe that, in its time, was the most famous restaurant dessert in America.

Lars liked the vagabond life of a skilled baker and moved to other restaurants before being hired in the early 1950s as Fulgenico Batista's pastry chef in Havana at the Cuban dictator's own private hotel. Jeff remembered that as a boy of three in Cuba, in the mornings he fed chopped meat to the hotel's turtles.

The family purchased property in Cuba, and Lars thought that executive baking on the island—known as the Pearl of the Antilles—might represent a final stop on his itinerant professional baking career. But in 1959, when Fidel Castro's revolution ousted Batista's government, the new Cuban Communist leader ordered foreigners off the island; Fidel had no need of a private pastry chef to whip up crème brûlée or bake Linzer tortes.

The years continued, and Lars moved to Florida to open the classy Fontainebleau in Miami and to the Claremont Diner in Verona, New Jersey, one of the first home-baking, gourmet-style megadiners in America.

Jeff wanted to learn more of the baking trade, and father and son returned to Denmark. Lars instructed Jeff to taste the baked goods of his native Denmark. Jeff said, "They don't make bread and pastries like this in America." Lars replied, "Why don't you stay here and find out how the Danes do it?"

Jeff stayed and learned the language. He spent the next three and a half years in apprenticeship, training full-time at the famous Restaurant Industry Hotel School in Copenhagen. Upon graduation, he became the pastry chef at the new Sheraton Hotel in Copenhagen, the first American-style hotel to open in northern Europe.

After three years, he decided to open his own bakery in Denmark. He met with a local accountant and learned that the taxes would cut into any profit the bakery generated. He realized then "that if I chose to remain in Denmark, in business for myself, my bakery would become my wife."

BACK IN THE UNITED STATES

In 1976, master pastry chef Jeff Jensen returned to the United States. He hired a baker's agent and insisted on working at a place where quality baking was paramount. He started at Pierce's 1894 Restaurant located in Elmira Heights, New York, in the Finger Lakes region. This was an award-winning restaurant operated by the Pierce family, and here Jensen flourished. He baked breads, pastries, and fancy cakes for weddings.

He stayed three years, but in that time experienced the reality of what his career would be like in the future as a pastry chef. He said, "A pastry chef is always a dead-end job, no matter how successful you are. There's no ladder of success to climb, no place higher up in the organization to go. You're always the pastry chef."

A different opportunity arose when Mövenpik, a fast-food restaurant concept from Switzerland, decided to enter the American market. After a test operation, the Swiss chain opened in New York City and, years later, in other U.S. locations. Mövenpik asked Jeff to develop the baking manuals, the written recipes that determine the ingredients, baking times, and presentation style of the baked items. For Jeff, writing the manuals proved to be one small step out of the everyday baking regimen.

Over the next few years, Jeff continued to work at individual restaurants and then for a large New Jersey catering company with a 20,000-square-foot commissary. In addition to supervising the baking, he was also in charge of laundry, adding another nonbaking skill to his resume.

COME TO THE CARNEGIE

In 1988, Harold Jaffe, the manager of the Carnegie Deli's Secaucus restaurant, who had worked with Jensen before, needed someone with commissary management experience to handle the basement operation, then supplying the Seventh Avenue flagship and also the new satellite delis. Jensen recognized the Carnegie Deli name and knew of its high-quality reputation. He also liked the idea that the position was managing a total food operation, curing meats, and also some baking. Jensen's first step was to improve the cheesecake recipe.

When the Carnegie Deli restaurant in Secaucus closed, Jensen recommended to Milton Parker that the commissary needed more space. Part of the reason for the expansion was due to the opening of the Carnegie Deli's new back room.

The Carnegie Deli found larger production space in Manhattan on Avenue D in a 6,000-square-foot USDA-approved space once occupied by the White Star Food Company. Parker asked Jensen if he was satisfied with the new, larger production space. Jensen replied, "Milton, we're going to grow, and soon I'll need a larger plant."

By the mid-1990s, the commissary supplied product to the Seventh Avenue deli only, because the other U.S. branches had closed. Jensen realized that without the other branches in operation, he had to find new business to replace the satellite accounts.

Jensen's problem: How to utilize the capacity of the commissary? How to expand the Carnegie Deli business without continuing the unprofitable business model of opening other regional delicatessens and failing in the process? The solution: wholesale.

Fortunately, Milton Parker encouraged Jensen to embark upon a small test market to search for new wholesale accounts. The baby steps that Jeff Jensen took to expand his operation would transform the revenue and profitability of the Carnegie Deli.

Jeff Can Get It for You Wholesale

Jensen had spent many years in restaurants and knew of an inexpensive method to announce the opening of the fledgling wholesale operation; he would use table tents, small, folded-over cardboard placecards set out on the tables at the Carnegie Deli. The card featured photos of the cakes available to eat at the deli and also a picture of the cheesecake gift box available by FedEx. At the bottom of the card, it was mentioned that wholesale accounts were welcome for all Carnegie Deli products.

Jensen received his first wholesale inquiry from a restaurant soon after the cards appeared on the tables. The buyer asked one provocative question: "Could the restaurant advertise the fact that this was authentic Carnegie Deli product?"

Jensen decided that any wholesale account could announce: "We serve Carnegie Deli meats or cheesecake." But they could not advertise in headlines on the tops of menus: "Carnegie Deli Sandwiches" or "Carnegie Deli Desserts," and include dishes made from their own kitchens, or products bought from other supply houses.

In 1999, under its own corporate name, the Carnegie Deli commissary moved to renovated and sparkling USDA-certified premises in Carlstadt, New Jersey, an entire building of 22,000 square feet. Jensen was now in charge of a huge operation and looked for ways to increase the sales of cured meats and also cheesecakes.

By this time, the Internet had proved a successful method for mail-order sales. Jensen set up a cheesecake 800 number on the Carnegie Deli web site. Everyone in the country could buy a 6-inch, 8-inch, or 12-inch cheesecake and have it arrive the next day. Sales skyrocketed.

Also, more regional food distributors received calls from local restaurants and hotels, asking if they carried Carnegie Deli pastrami, corned beef, or tongue. Soon, more of these food brokers contacted the commissary.

Jensen utilized an interesting three-callback system to weed out the Looky-Lous from the more serious and interested wholesale buyers. He kept three piles of telephone slips; first-time callers, second-time callers, and third-timers. He called back the last group because they really wanted the product. Experience had proved that if he called back a first-time caller, that person was doing price and delivery research and had only mild interest in making a purchase.

Another benefit to having a professional, state-of-the-art food preparation plant is that it allows potential new accounts to visit the commissary. New wholesale accounts are also encouraged to spend time working behind the deli counter in New York.

Jensen said, "We invite the new accounts to come to the commissary and view firsthand the cuts of meat that we buy from meatpacking houses. Then, we demonstrate how we cure the meats with the brine machine and how we bake the cheesecakes by hand. We're proud to demonstrate the high quality standard."

THE SATISFIED EXECUTIVE

Jeff Jensen sits in his large office on the second floor of the commissary. In the outside room, operators answer the daily 800 calls, sending cheesecakes to every state in the United States. On the first floor is an immaculately clean USDA-approved production facility replete with cold rooms and a large smoker. The commissary is humming.

Jensen praised management. He said, "Milton Parker has great deli sense. He loves the Carnegie and the deli business.

The two best things that ever happened to the Carnegie are Milton and Sandy. Sandy, too, has become a real deli man."

The wholesale operation, which continues to grow annually, is the growth center for the future. Jensen described the reasons for the lack of success from the past satellite attempts. He said, "It was impossible to copy the Carnegie Deli in other cities. But, today, why shouldn't we let everyone else try to become a Carnegie Deli by giving them the Carnegie meats and the cakes? We can't prepare the sandwiches or serve the cheesecakes. We can only give them our great product."

Reflecting on his career, he admitted, "I saw the writing on the wall while working for Mövenpik. I witnessed the success of serving many places and many accounts out of one central commissary. I knew then I had to break away from being tagged a pastry chef, or I would be handling a rolling pin for the rest of my life."

Jeff Jensen and the Marvelous Cheesecake

DESSERTS OF THE DELI WORLD

The desserts of the delicatessen world are not many, but the assortment is varied enough to please any palate. Historically, Eastern Europeans living on small farms and in small towns were limited in what their meager food budgets could purchase. There were rarely enough cash or barter options for fresh or dried fruits, the staples of dessert making.

Sweet items appeared at dinners honoring happy times during Jewish holidays like Hanukkah, Passover, or Purim. For a sweet treat during or after a big meal, delicatessens offer cheesecake, rugelach, noodle or kugel pudding, blintzes, and apple strudel.

Cheesecake

Cheesecake dates back to ancient Greece. The cream cheesecake you make at home comes from old Polish recipes that were brought to this country years ago. Those ancient Polish recipes used *kvak*, a full-fat cream cheese that is similar to the American cream cheese used today in the cakes. As a staple, cheese was plentiful and not expensive, which is the main reason it has been passed down through European generations.

To make the famous Carnegie Deli cheesecake at home, follow the recipe on pages 146 and 147.

Blintzes

Blintzes can be traced back to as early as ancient Persia when thin pancakes were made during lean times and served with fruit or cheese. Filled pancakes span all cultures: the crepe in France, *blinis* or *blintchikis* from Russia, manicotti from Italy, and *palacinky*, the Czech dessert crepes filled with chocolate, jam, or ice cream.

What distinguishes blintzes from the other pancake forms is that they are usually thicker, larger, and fried. Also, cheese is a prime ingredient for the blintzes compared with fruits from other cultures.

The Carnegie Deli blintz recipe is on page 150.

Strudel

Strudel means "whirlpool" in German. The distinguishing feature of a good strudel is its flakiness, which originated with the Greeks and their perfecting phyllo (the word for leaf in Greek) dough. The dough was the base for the honeyed sweet baklava, served in Greek restaurants around the world.

Eastern Europeans took the thin dough and filled it with apples, raisins, and nuts. Later, cherry would become the second most favorite strudel preference after apple.

Rugelach

Rugelach means "little horns." These are delicious cookies in their distinctive crescent shape often made for Purim and other holidays. The rugelach cookie is notable for its cream cheese dough and for the predominance of apricot. The Carnegie Deli recipe for these tasty bites is on page 148.

Noodle Pudding

Noodle pudding or *kugel* is a popular mainstay of delicatessen fare. It is served warm (sometimes with cream), and some enjoy it cold. Similar to many other Eastern European–origin sweets, the pudding contains apples and nuts. Want to make a delicious noodle pudding at home? Try the Carnegie Deli recipe on page 149.

DESSERT RECIPES

CHEESECAKE

If you want to make this world-famous delicacy at home, follow the recipe.

Cookie Crust

1 cup all-purpose flour
¼ cup sugar
1 teaspoon grated lemon rind
½ teaspoon vanilla extract
1 egg yolk
1 stick (½ cup) unsalted butter, chilled and cut into ¼-inch bits

Cheese Filling

1¼ pounds softened cream cheese
¾ cup sugar
1½ tablespoons flour
1½ teaspoons lemon juice
1½ teaspoons vanilla extract
3 eggs plus 1 egg yolk
2 tablespoons heavy cream

Making the Crust

1. Place the flour, sugar, grated lemon rind, vanilla extract, egg yolk, and butter in a large mixing bowl. With your fingertips, rub the ingredients together until they are well mixed and can be gathered into a ball. Dust with a little flour, wrap in waxed paper, and refrigerate for at least 1 hour.
2. Butter and flour the bottom of a 9-inch by 2-inch springform pan. Roll out a piece of dough to cover bottom. Dough should be as thick as for a normal sugar cookie (¼ inch). Bake in a pre-heated 350-degree oven to a light brown color. Remove from the oven and cool. Butter the sides of the pan. Roll out and line the sides of the pan with more of the cookie dough. Trim excess dough from the edges.

CHEESECAKE (CONTINUED)

Making the Filling

Place the cream cheese in a large mixing bowl and beat vigorously with a wooden spoon until it is creamy and smooth. Beat in the sugar, a few tablespoons at a time, and when it is well incorporated, beat in the flour, lemon juice, vanilla, eggs and egg yolk, and heavy cream. No lumps, please!

Baking: Step One

Preheat the oven to 485 to 500 degrees. Oven should be hot to enhance color. Pour the filling into the cookie-dough-lined pan, and bake in the center of the oven until the top is golden brown. The cake should also start to rise slightly. Remove from the oven. Cool for 30 minutes and set oven to 350 degrees.

Baking: Step Two

After 30 minutes, return cheesecake to the oven for a final baking. This procedure will set the cake. Remember that the cheesecake is like a pudding. When the cake is bouncy in the center and slightly risen in the middle as well as on the sides, it's finished.

Notes

If you bake too long, the cake will crack and be firm. If you remove the cake too soon, the cake will tend to be soft in the center. It's very similar to baking a flan or a quiche. Time will vary, due to the variance of each oven (usually 25 to 40 minutes).

Cool at least 2 hours before attempting to remove from the pan. It is best to refrigerate overnight and serve at nearly room temperature. Always cut with a hot, wet knife. Fresh fruit makes a great complement.

It usually takes a couple of tries to get it just right.

Rugelach Cookies
(Makes about 150 Cookies)

These sweet treats have been a delicious staple in delicatessens for years. The horn- or crescent-shaped cookies are ideal as little desserts after a heavy meal or served with coffee or tea.

Dough Ingedients

2½ pounds cream cheese
2½ pounds butter
1½ pounds powdered sugar
2½ pounds all-purpose flour
¾ ounce baking powder
1 teaspoon vanilla
Lemon zest to taste
Crushed hazelnuts and raisins
Cinnamon sugar
2 egg yolks, beaten

Franzipan Ingredients

1 pound sugar
1 pound almond paste
1 pound cinnamon sugar

Instructions

1. Have the first seven ingredients at room temperature. Mix into a smooth dough. Refrigerate for an hour.
2. Roll dough on a lightly floured dough cloth into ½-inch thickness.
3. Coat dough with franzipan mix.
4. Cover dough with crushed hazelnuts, raisins, and cinnamon sugar and then roll all ingredients lightly with a rolling pin.
5. Cut dough lengthwise with a pizza cutter into 2½-inch wide strips.
6. Roll each strip like a jelly roll.
7. Cut the strips into ¾-inch cookies and brush lightly with egg.
8. Sprinkle on more cinnamon sugar.
9. Bake in a 375-degree oven until lightly brown (about 25 to 30 minutes).

To Serve

Offer up a plate of cookies to friends and family.

NOODLE PUDDING WITH APPLES
(Serves Six)

Who doesn't love the taste of a hot noodle pudding and the aroma of baked apples? With this *lochen kugel* recipe, you'll be able to serve pudding as a dessert or as a side dish.

Ingredients

2 eggs, beaten
3 tablespoons sugar
¼ teaspoon cinnamon
Salt to taste
½ pound broad noodles, cooked as directed on the package and drained
1 cup tart apples, shredded
¼ cup raisins
½ cup walnuts, chopped
4 tablespoons melted butter

Instructions

1. Combine eggs, sugar, cinnamon, and salt.
2. Add the mixture to the noodles.
3. Add the apples, raisins, walnuts, and melted butter.
4. Mix thoroughly.
5. Place mixture in a well-greased 1½-quart casserole.
6. Bake at 400 degrees for about 1 hour (until brown on top).

To Serve

Cut into squares and serve heated with cream.

CHEESE BLINTZES
(Makes Three)

This Eastern European crepe is a delicious dessert or can be served as a light meal.

Ingredients for the Crepes

2 eggs
1 cup milk
2 tablespoons olive oil
¾ cup all-purpose flour
½ teaspoon salt
½ cup butter

Instructions for the Crepes

1. Combine eggs, milk, and oil, then add the flour and the salt. Mix and refrigerate for 30 to 40 minutes.
2. Melt a teaspoon of butter in a thick skillet and pour in enough batter to thinly cover the bottom of the pan.
3. At medium heat, cook each crepe until slightly brown on the bottom, then tap it out onto a paper towel.
4. Repeat until three crepes are made.

Ingredients for the Filling

½ cup cottage cheese
8 ounces cream cheese
2 tablespoons sugar
1 teaspoon vanilla
1 egg
Matzoh brei (for thickening)

Instructions

1. Mix all ingredients and refrigerate until ready to use.
2. Put ⅓ of the cheese mixture into each crepe and roll to form three cylinders.
3. Sauté the crepes gently in olive oil on a low flame for 5 or 6 minutes, or until lightly browned on the outside.

To Serve

Serve with applesauce or sour cream.

APPLE STRUDEL
(Serves Eight)

This recipe is one that Carnegie Deli master baker Jeff Jensen per-fected during his baking apprenticeship in Denmark.

Ingredients

Puff pastry dough (Make your own or buy from the frozen food section of the supermarket.)
½ cup cake crumbs, ground fine
1½ cups filbert nuts, chopped fine
2 pounds apples (Granny Smith or any other tart variety), peeled, quartered, and then cut into eighths
3 tablespoons cinnamon sugar
¼ cup raisins, washed (*Tip:* The raisins can be marinated in white wine overnight.)
1 egg, beaten
Icing sugar

Instructions

1. Heat oven to 420 degrees.
2. With a rolling pin, roll the dough out the to ⅛-inch thickness and 12 inches in length.
3. Place the dough in a lightly buttered baking dish.
4. Sprinkle the ground cake crumbs and filbert nuts down the center of the dough.
5. Cover the mixture with apples.
6. Sprinkle the cinnamon sugar and add the raisins.
7. Brush one edge of the dough with egg.
8. Fold both sides over the filling and brush with egg again.
9. Bake for 35 to 40 minutes, until the strudel is baked through.
10. After baking, dust with icing sugar or glaze lightly with apricot puree and coat with vanilla-flavored fondant.

To Serve

Cut into portions and serve warm.

WALTER BELL, COUNTERMAN: "CONSTRUCTING THE BIG SANDWICH"

Walter Bell has been making delicious sandwiches at the Carnegie Deli for 24 years. He remembers that his first week working at the deli was the second week of July 1979.

Bell came to New York City from a small town in western Pennsylvania, and he had never before tasted or seen New York deli food. He started out at Henry's, a restaurant four doors down from Katz's Deli on Houston Street. When Henry's closed, he had the skills to apply for a counterman's job at the Carnegie.

Bell has seen the size of the sandwiches inch up each year. "Leo Steiner began offering the first big sandwich. Then, Mr. Parker said to me, 'Walter, we're going higher.' And we did. Sandy took it up a notch, too. A combination might contain three pounds of meat and be a foot in height when the onion, lettuce, tomato, and coleslaw are piled on."

The term *counterman* dates back at least to 1853, but in New York the word had a specific association with the trained sandwich makers who worked the front counters of delicatessens, sandwich shops, and coffee shops. These food service artists required two skills: the talent for taking sandwich orders with their many permutations of meats, fish, type of bread, vegetables, dressings, and so on, and—without looking frequently at the written orders—turning out and wrapping these in quick time. Office workers had a short break for lunch, and they wanted their orders fast. Only trained countermen, union members of Local #100, could get these people in and out, and also take care of the orders of the seated patrons.

Bell is sometimes the first and only Carnegie Deli employee whom customers see when they come in for a takeout sandwich. Many are tourists who want to take a sandwich to eat al fresco in Central Park (four short blocks away).

Often, he will be quizzed about the cured meats, and he doesn't mind offering a taste so the customer can decide between a corned beef, tongue, or pastrami. He accommodates all sandwich requests and will serve the cured meats or chopped liver on white bread (even putting on mayonnaise). However, he will put forward that these sandwiches taste better on rye bread and the diners usually go along with his suggestion.

Bell stated that the key to making a big Carnegie Deli sandwich is in the slicing. After all the fat is trimmed, the meat is sliced thin and immediately placed piece by piece on top of a fresh slice of rye bread. To build the big sandwich, the trick is to start placing the slices from the ends into the middle setting a slice on the right and then one on the left. Gradually, a mound appears in the middle from the careful layering until the sandwich is about 4½ inches high (it's a visual call; there are no rulers at the counter). Then, the top slice of bread is set on the meat and should balance on the crown without toppling off the plate.

The combinations—which bring gasps of shock and delight—rise up to 12 inches and are pierced with a long, wooden skewer.

Bell is philosophical about the size of the Carnegie's offerings: "It's not the amount of meat, it's the taste. The important thing is that the customer should have a nice sandwich."

On his 25th anniversary in July 2004, Walter Bell continued to make the customers happy with "a nice sandwich."

FERNANDO PEREZ, COOK: "COOKING THE CARNEGIE WAY"

Fernando Perez, a senior cook at the Carnegie Deli, started out as a pharmacist in Colombia. After working for 10 years, he realized that there were too many trained pharmacists in his country and decided to immigrate to America in the mid-1970s.

In the United States, he learned that to continue professionally in the pharmacy trade, he would have to study again to be certified. He did not speak English well, and the idea of more course work in a foreign language proved discouraging. He looked for other work, any kind of work.

In June 1980, with no real skills, and with bills to pay, he accepted a job at the Carnegie Deli as a dishwasher. Leo Steiner assured him that the deli's policy was to promote from within. Fernando concentrated on improving his English-language skills and pointed his career to learning the more interesting tasks in the kitchen.

After two years of washing dishes, he was promoted to an assistant cook with preparation responsibilities. His mentor was John, the head cook, who recognized that Fernando possessed excellent work habits and also the ability to memorize quickly (like prescriptions in a pharmacy) the various and diverse ingredients that went into each dish.

Fernando assumed the cook's role when John retired. The duties included making all the hot food on the menu from breakfast to dinners, including preparing blintzes. Today, he is the one who teaches new assistants how to maintain the high-quality food and how to cook the generous portions that are the hallmark of every Carnegie Deli meal.

Naturally, the deli food was new and exotic to him, not the kind of cuisine found in Colombia. But to echo the former Levy's rye bread advertising, you don't have to be Jewish to cook delicious deli food. He says that his wife prefers corned beef to the spicy pastrami.

He praised Leo Steiner for having made a connection with the people and compliments Milton Parker and Sandy Levine for continuing that tradition.

The ability to keep all the meals in his head is a continuation of his previous—and now long-ago—pharmacist training. In fact, he named off the ingredients and cooking directions for the many appetizer and entree recipes in this book without ever referring to recipe cards.

Fernando gave up the mortar and pestle for the ladle and whisk. For 24 years, he has worked in the kitchen, rising to the status of head Carnegie Deli cook. He said, "I'm happy here. Happy to be cooking."

JOEL SIEGEL, DINER:
"LOVING THE DELI LIFE"

One of the loyal celebrity regulars at the Carnegie Deli has been ABC's *Good Morning America's* six-time Emmy-award-winning Joel Siegel, a frequent diner at the restaurant, starting in the late 1970s and continuing up to the present. He narrated a wonderful deli journey from the used pickle barrels of Los Angeles to the cured pastrami of New York City.

When Joel was four years old, his Uncle Muttie took him to eat for the first time in Canter's Delicatessen, located then in the Boyle Heights section of Los Angeles. The famous deli moved in 1948 to North Fairfax near Beverly Boulevard in the more prosperous west side, where it is today.

While Joel dined on tasty tidbits of chopped liver, kasha varnishkas, and corned beef, Uncle Muttie hinted in reverent tones of more delicious and exotic delicatessen treats awaiting the boy "back east."

Joel's other childhood connection to the deli world occurred on the days his mother took him to Brooklyn Avenue,

LA's ethnic counterpart of New York's old Delancey Street. On these outings, while she shopped for gefilte fish or brisket, he amused himself by climbing inside the used pickle barrels that aired out in the rear of the barrel maker's store. He wondered for years how his mother could always recognize where he had done the mischief making.

Joel attended UCLA and said he must have eaten a few meals at Canter's and perhaps once at Nate 'n Al's in Beverly Hills. At least he had enough deli experience to laugh at the hilarious world-is-coming-to-an-end parody in comic Lenny Bruce's classic bit, "The Day Canter's Closed."

MANHATTAN

Fast-forward to 1972, when CBS invited Siegel to come to New York City and discuss a career change. The network put him up at the Hilton Hotel on Sixth Avenue across from the broadcast company's headquarters.

Manhattan at night was a scary place to a happy-go-lucky guy from sunny, drive-in-the-safety-of-your-car Los Angeles, and Siegel never ventured out after dark. But during daytime walks in the neighborhood, he spied the Stage Deli on Seventh Avenue. The cheesecakes in its window sang to him like the Sirens' song. For days, his head was filled with the sumptuous images of those soft and creamy white cakes, seductively crooning, "Come taste us. Come, Joel, partake of dessert paradise."

On his last evening in New York, he resolved to overcome fear of the city at night and visited the Stage Delicatessen. Here he ordered a piece of cheesecake and entered the gates of tummy-pleasing ecstasy.

In 1972, he arrived in New York to begin broadcasting work at CBS, and started frequenting the Stage Delicatessen. One night, he sat in between two recognizable music personalities, disk jockey Murray the K, the fifth Beatle, and Gian Carlo

Menotti, composer of *The Gift of the Magi*. Siegel wondered whether he should introduce the dissimilar music notables but decided to let them dine undisturbed.

CARNEGIE DELI TIME

Siegel first entered the Carnegie Deli sometime after the pastrami review in 1979. When he savored that first bite into the succulent, no-fat, cured meat sandwich, he knew that the Carnegie would become his deli of choice.

The Carnegie's Leo Steiner recognized him at the outset and, from that moment on, Siegel and the outgoing owner became fast friends. Part of Siegel's initiation into Steiner's exclusive club was the awarding of the celebrity person cloth napkin.

When Siegel came in alone, Steiner would scan the room looking for another celebrity. On one occasion, he sat Siegel next to one of the broadcaster's youthful idols, comic Morey Amsterdam, then in his late 70s. Amsterdam, who enjoyed a long career as comic and lyricist, is best remembered for his Buddy Sorrel character on television's *Dick Van Dyke* program. Much to the comedian's delight, Siegel sang the verses to a classic Amsterdam funny song, "Yukka Puck." The comedian said that Siegel was the "youngest" person who had ever remembered those long-forgotten lyrics.

Two of Siegel's most treasured moments in the Carnegie Deli involved Henny Youngman and Siegel's first wife, Jane (who died of cancer). Youngman asked the couple, "Would you like to see a photograph of my pride and joy?" When the Siegels nodded yes, Youngman handed them a picture of Pride furniture polish and Joy dishwashing liquid. Another time, Youngman said to Jane, "You're a pretty lady. I'm going to give you a *diam-ond* pin." He handed her a *dime on* a pin!

Siegel wrote the book to the musical *The First* about the life of Jackie Robinson. In the course of doing research, he chatted often with Tommy Lasorda, the ebullient Los Angeles Dodgers manager. As they were enjoying dinner together at the Carnegie, Lasorda patted his stomach and said, "I never had a meal at the Carnegie I did not love." Then, he smiled and added, "To tell the truth, I never had a meal *anywhere* I did not love."

In 1983, Siegel interviewed the famous New Orleans chef Paul Prudhomme (founder of K-Paul's Louisiana Kitchen), who had just come to New York after cooking for international dignitaries during an economic summit in Williamsburg, Virginia. Siegel said, "My friend Leo Steiner from the Carnegie was at the summit also." Prudhomme's face lit up like a baked Alaska. He said, "I loved Leo the first time I met him. He was in a nearby kitchen and I heard him shout, 'Don't touch my corned beef!' I knew this was a man serious about his food."

Siegel narrated a Carnegie story concerning his friend, the writer Michael Kramer, one of a group of writers who used to meet at the deli. Kramer was sent to Israel to do a story and the group decided to send him a Carnegie Deli salami to keep his spirits up. When Kramer went to the post office in Tel Aviv to pick up this treat, he discovered an empty brown wrapper and no salami. An Israeli postal worker said, "Even in Israel, we recognized the name of New York's famous Carnegie Deli. We knew from the shape what was inside, so we ate it. Delicious."

Siegel takes his young son Daniel into the restaurant to pass on the deli tradition of foods that originated among Eastern Europeans centuries ago. Often, after chatting with people from out of town, he will send over a free piece of cheesecake, keeping up Leo Steiner's tasting tradition.

Reflecting on his 25 years dining at the Carnegie Deli, he does have one favorite memory. Uncle Muttie from Los Angeles came to New York to visit his celebrated nephew. Siegel took him to the Carnegie Deli where his uncle was overwhelmed at the deli smells, the sights, and the animated crowd. The two ordered chopped liver, kasha varnishkas, and corned beef, and after tasting these delicacies, almost with tears of joy in his eyes, Uncle Muttie said, "This is deli heaven. I said long ago you would find it back east."

GENUINE BROOKLYN EGG CREAM RECIPE
by Michael Isaacson

History

This drink—once concocted by Brooklyn candy store owners with soda fountains for mixing egg creams, malteds, lime rickies, black and white sodas—used to contain both eggs and cream to fatten up skinny Brooklyn kids. Today, this classic recipe contains neither. If you follow the directions below, you will experience a libation that will make you crave seconds of this nectar of the Flatbush gods.

Ingredients and Measurements

- Enough whole milk (not skimmed or fat free) to fill the bottom of an 8-ounce Coke glass before it flares out. (First secret: Milk must be in the freezer until it is "chippy" cold; not frozen, but cold enough to have chips of frozen milk floating. This gives the egg cream its creaminess.)
- *Chocolate syrup*: Popular wisdom has always suggested Fox's U-Bet brand syrup as the best, but Bell brand or any comparable fully sweet chocolate syrup will do. (Caveat: Hershey's semi-sweet will not do!) Two full squeezes from a fountain pump (about 3 to 4 generous tablespoons) should do nicely.
- *Seltzer water*: The best kind is from a well-charged fountain or a seltzer bottle with a siphon. But in a pinch, ice-cold pure seltzer water from a bottle may be used. (*Note*: No carbonated water or mineral water with added salts.) Just

enough to fill the glass and never use a paper or plastic cup for the genuine experience.

- *A mixing spoon:* A metal fountain spoon about 10 inches long.

Procedure

1. Gently pump or spoon in the chocolate syrup but be careful not to run any on the sides of the glass. If this should happen, immediately end the attempt and try again.
2. Remove the milk container from the freezer and fill up the bottom, unflared section of the Coke glass with the chippy cold milk.
3. This next step is crucial to success. While someone else is briskly pouring in the seltzer (Advanced technicians may be able to pour and mix simultaneously, but this is certainly beyond the skills of neophytes.), gently bounce the spoon up and down, thereby mixing the syrup and the seltzer on the bottom of the glass.
4. The milk above it will elegantly and independently rise in a pristine white froth to the top. **Do not stir under any circumstances!** This would cause the milk to join the other ingredients and all you will have to show for your efforts is a pathetic chocolate soda with milk. *Pffeh!*

Brooklyn-born Dr. Michael Isaacson grew up eating Carnegie Deli pastrami sandwiches and Mrs. Stahl's knishes, and, of course, drinking egg creams. He has been successful as a Hollywood composer of film and television music. He is also the conductor of the Israel Pops, and his symphonic music can be heard as part of the permanent exhibit at the Museum of Jewish Heritage in Battery Park, New York City (www.michaelisaacson.com).

5. If using a fountain, advanced technicians may add a quick backhand of carbon dioxide to add a *zetz* to the gassy seltzer.
6. A genuine Brooklyn egg cream is a cold, sweet, dark chocolaty drink with a creamy white head. This is your ultimate goal. Practice, practice, practice, and serve it with a thick, crisp, salted pretzel rod if you can.

SUSAN PALMACCIO, WAITRESS: "WHEN SHE'S SMILING"

"Don't you ever smile?" asked an innocent Carnegie Deli customer of Susan Palmaccio, a waitress from the old school who started working in the legendary Schrafft's, the famous New York City restaurant chain memorialized in a poem by W. H. Auden.

The response from the unsmiling server cut the air with a saberlike thrust. "What did you come here for? To eat or to see teeth?"

The out-of-towner, who was accustomed to the back home and generically polite, "Hi, I'm Mardee, your waitress," was stunned by the tart comeback.

Undaunted, the customer continued, "Well, do you smile at all?"

"Smiles cause wrinkles," Susan replied with a look that could slice thick pastrami thin. Finally, the customer got the message: This waitress was not going to spout pleasantries and perform like a trained seal.

Susan has worked for more than 40 years as a New York City waitress, and her tolerance for lip or sass from customers is nil. She admits to having a quick temper, saying, "I will not be put down. I never smile until I do my job. I'm not paid to smile."

In order to raise her children, she often had to do two or three waitressing jobs. She worked in the old Zum Zum restaurant in New York and for many years at Wolff's, another busy delicatessen on West 57th Street, now closed. She's been a regular at the Carnegie for 15 years.

Susan distinguished the everyday arrival of Carnegie customers: The breakfast eaters are perky and in a hurry to get to work or eat one last Carnegie meal before they catch a plane. At lunchtime, it's filled with tourists who are animated and having a good time. At night, the dinner patrons are laid-back and unrushed. Often, there is an elderly man in town on business eating alone, ordering a traditional deli dish like flanken or matzoh ball soup.

Susan believes that there is a basis for her irritability. In the old days, servers were forbidden to answer back to rude customers. She said, "I had to bite my tongue a lot in the past."

Staff and management are aware of Susan's short fuse. The other servers keep a vigilant eye out for their caustic coworker, often moving swiftly to take an order or clean off a table, especially if they spot fire breath coming from Susan's mouth.

Many will say that Susan's bark is worse than her bite. Once she takes the order and delivers it, she's all smiles to the customers. And then she'll embark on a little fun chat with the guests. "They laugh. I laugh. I can disguise a little zip with some typical New York remarks," she said.

She praised the Carnegie for being a superb quality restaurant that is well organized and efficient. The head waitress hands out the schedules, and the lunchtime servers in the back room pool tips. Susan was pleased by the tip-sharing agreement, which resulted in newfound teamwork. "We work like a train here. If someone's busy, I'll come in behind and help out. We don't have busboys here, so it's important to clear the tables and have the next party seated," she said.

Asked what was the worst event that ever happened between her and a customer, she replied, "Once at Schrafft's I busted a plate over a lady's head." And she said it with a big smile on her face.

THE DELICATESSEN QUIZ

1. When you ask, "Waiter, what's a fly doing in my soup" his response?
   a. "The backstroke."
   b. "Fishing for noodles."
   c. "What am I? Your Internet search engine?"
   d. "Ask the fly, I'm too busy making a living."

2. What items are often on a deli table when you arrive?
   a. A cup of crayons.
   b. Sour pickles and sour tomatoes.
   c. Pickled beets and pickled carrots.
   d. Flat bread and garlic butter.

3. What is found on traditional deli walls?
   a. Old menus with yesterday's prices.
   b. Photographs of the Brooklyn Dodgers' 1955 World Series team.
   c. *Shtetl* life from Eastern Europe.
   d. Signed celebrity photographs.

4. A hint of a great deli is the smell of?
   a. Cured and salted meats.
   b. Cakes baked on the premises.
   c. Freshly made salads.
   d. All of the above.

5. What are the usual names of New York deli owners?
   a. Pierre, Augustin, and Jean-Claude.
   b. Winston, Baxter, and Chauncey.
   c. Milton, Leo, and Sandy.
   d. Ingvar, Odin, and Knute.

6. What is a traditional pastrami sandwich order?
   a. White bread with mayo, litchi nut paste, and India relish.
   b. Toasted English muffin, dried pimientos, and apple butter.
   c. Rye bread with Russian dressing.
   d. Pita pockets with chutney, Dijon mustard, and chicken fat.

(continued)

THE DELICATESSEN QUIZ (CONTINUED)

7. What will you find hanging on overhead racks in some delis?
   a. Purim holiday puppets.
   b. Chili pepper strings.
   c. Halvah candies.
   d. Salamis.

8. What will a waiter or waitress at a New York deli be wearing?
   a. Shirt, tie, pants, and a vest.
   b. Bermuda shorts and a logo T-shirt.
   c. Tuxedo.
   d. Costumes from *Fiddler on the Roof.*

9. What was the historic New York deli flooring?
   a. Turkish area rugs.
   b. Small, white octagonal tiles.
   c. Pine board planking.
   d. Linoleum with a multifloral design border.

10. What's the only phrase you'll hear at the Carnegie Deli?
    a. "It's so quiet here, it's like being in a library."
    b. "Have you ever seen such tiny portions?"
    c. "I'm stuffed. It was delicious."
    d. "I loved the sushi and the sashimi."

Scoring:

9 to 10:   You are a connoisseur of deli food.
5 to 8:   You have some tasty deli experiences in your past.
Below 5:   You need to make more trips to your nearest deli.

Answers: 1a, 2b, 3d, 4d, 5c, 6c, 7d, 8a, 9b, 10c

IT'S CLOSING TIME

It is a time for endings, and like the Carnegie Deli, which shuts its doors at 4 A.M., this book, too, must close.

Our wish has been like a delicious meal at the deli, you have been fulfilled reading about the history and the biographies of the many people who made the Carnegie Deli famous. We hope that you enjoyed the many delicious recipes and learned a little something new about delicatessen lore and the deli business.

If you want to order any item from the Carnegie Deli menu, telephone (800) 334-5606. The menu is online at the web site address: www.carnegiedeli.com. All food will be shipped by FedEx to arrive the next day. The delivery comes with easy-to-follow heating instructions.

For cheesecakes, you can telephone (877) 898-3354 from 8 A.M. to 5 P.M. (EST) or order online at www.carnegiedeli.com.

Prospective wholesale buyers should telephone Jeff Jensen at (201) 507-5557 for information about buying the cured meats and other deli products. Remember, you can tour the facility in New Jersey to see how they make the cured meats and the cheesecakes.

You can also give a Carnegie Deli gift certificate by either purchasing it online or whenever you stop in the deli.

A private dining room is available for parties or meetings. Telephone and ask for the banquet manager.

Thinking of a clever product introduction or food promotion? Then consider the Carnegie Deli as the perfect spot. Telephone and speak with Sandy Levine.

To thank the reader for purchasing this book, we have included a coupon for a **free slice of Carnegie Deli cheesecake** at the back of the book. Cut the coupon out, stick it in your wallet, and present it to our restaurant server the next time you come into the deli.

Finally, remember, when you're eating in the Carnegie Deli, you're not just taking a bite out of the best-tasting deli food in America, you're taking a 67-year trip back in time to old New York.

Enjoy.

MILTON PARKER AND ALLYN FREEMAN

New York City
June 2004

ABOUT THE ARTIST

I painted my first oil painting when I was six years old. My father's best friend, who became my godfather was a very fine artist. His name is James P. Barbarite and he had exhibited in New York with Reginald Marsh and Edward Hopper back in the 1930s.

He would babysit me when my parents went to a movie or somewhere children could not go. I would sit as still as could be and watch him paint, which made his babysitting job quite easy.

I can remember how fascinated I was seeing the painting he was working on develop before my young eyes. He always worked from nature whether it was a still life or a portrait. He inspired me to become an artist, thus my first attempt at age six. He remained my mentor and was always there for me with encouragement and advice (when asked).

Later I attended the School of Industrial Arts in Manhattan. Soon the Korean War broke out and the draft was approaching. I enlisted in the Air Force and had a career as a Contracting Officer. I painted on and off doing simple paintings that took maybe 20 or 30 hours to complete.

After retiring from the Air Force in 1986, I decided to paint full-time and made a success of it. One gallery would buy everything I painted. After a few years, I decided that it would be best to paint one really good picture than many mediocre ones.

I've always used the aid of photographs in my work because I knew I could do a more detailed painting that way. After several years of experimentation, I came upon an ideal subject matter.

Newsstand images are my focus for now. I have over two hundred source photographs of newsstands taken on the many street corners of New York City. They are constantly changing. The attendants are selling papers, candy, magazines, maps, and more recently, jewelry and trinkets. Some are even selling lottery tickets.

That's a lot of things to paint in one picture so I spend up to three months working a minimum of 50 hours per week on each painting.

Some of the magazines on prominent display usually hang down from the top of the stand. The selection is not always to my liking so I create my own. I pretend that I'm in charge of the stand and place certain current magazines that we all can identify with across the top.

This allows me to paint my selection instead of what the source photograph offers.

The candy bars are painted from real wrappers to get the minute detail. I like to add a little trompe l'oeil here and there that may not be in the source material to make the painting more realistic than the photograph. I like to give my pictures a lot of depth, which I find gives the viewer a desire to touch my work (and they sometimes do). It's a great thrill for me to see someone try to grab one of my candy bars off the canvas. Recently while exhibiting with the Helander Gallery at Art Miami, a very welcome comment came from the exquisite human figure painter, Bernardo Torrens of Spain. His spontaneous reaction to seeing one of my newsstands was "Ken, it is American and superrealistic."

Superreal. Superrealist. I've heard those names before.

I don't associate myself with any movement of art. I'm not influenced by any particular style.

I like Rembrandt and I also like Hopper.

I just try to make my paintings look as real as I can. When my works are reproduced, they look like photographs, but then all real things reproduced by the camera look like photographs.

KEN KEELEY

"FREE SLICE OF CHEESECAKE"

- Cut out this coupon and place it in your wallet.
- On your next visit to the Carnegie Deli, present this coupon to a server.
- You will receive one **free slice of delicious cheesecake.**
- Thanks for buying the book.

With Love from CARNEGIE®
DELICATESSEN & RESTAURANT

authorized signature

Void if altered, transferred, sold, reproduced, or exchanged. One per customer.
The Carnegie Deli reserves the right to terminate this promotion at any time.

BIG HITS AT

west side specialties

Served with cole slaw

PRIME BRISKET OF BEEF POT ROAST
In rich brown gravy with potato
pancake and fresh vegetable ... 19.95

BAKED MEATLOAF Mushroom gravy,
choice of potato and fresh vegetable ... 15.95

HUNGARIAN GOULASH Served over
broad noodles and fresh vegetable ... 15.95

BAKED SHORT RIBS OF BEEF With baked
Idaho potato and fresh vegetable ... 18.95

BOILED BEEF FLANKEN
Choice of potato and fresh vegetable ... 18.95

SAUTEED CHICKEN LIVERS
Choice of potato and fresh vegetable ... 15.95

ROAST VERMONT TURKEY PLATTER
With giblet gravy, candied sweet potato,
cranberry sauce and fresh vegetable ... 19.95

JUMBO TURKEY DRUMSTICK or WING
With candied sweet potato, cranberry
sauce and fresh vegetable ... 17.95

HOT TONGUE PLATTER
In our famous sweet and sour gravy with
potato pancake and fresh vegetable ... 18.95

**ROUMANIAN CHICKEN PAPRIKASH,
EN CASSEROLE**
Served with rice and fresh vegetable ... 17.95

ROAST HALF CHICKEN With stuffing, candied
sweet potato and fresh vegetable ... 15.95

BOILED HALF SPRING CHICKEN
A traditional favorite, with boiled
potato and fresh vegetable ... 15.95

CORNED BEEF OR PASTRAMI HASH
Prepared with our famous
corned beef or pastrami
and made only to your order ... 16.95
With fried egg ... 17.95

STUFFED DERMA (KISHKA) With fresh
vegetable, kasha varnishkas and gravy ... 15.95

MILT'S FRESH GARLIC CHICKEN - 1/2 a chicken cut in succulent
pieces and broiled with fresh garlic and special seasonings
choice of potato and fresh vegetable ... 16.95

Potato pancake substitution	Extra 2.00

HALF SPRING CHICKEN
In the pot with
matzoh ball,
noodles,
consomme,
fresh vegetable
and cole slaw
19.95

MIDNIGHT SPECIAL
All beef
knockwurst, with
baked beans
and sauerkraut
11.95

MILTON'S BOILED BEEF FLANKEN
In the pot with
matzoh ball,
noodles,
consomme,
fresh vegetable
and cole slaw
19.95

MILLIE'S STUFFED CABBAGE ROUMANIAN STYLE
In sweet and
sour sauce, with
boiled potato,
fresh vegetable
and cole slaw
17.95